God's Messengers

God's Messengers

BY
A. M. DEIGLORIAM

WIPF & STOCK · Eugene, Oregon

GOD'S MESSENGERS

Copyright © 2021 A. M. Deigloriam. All rights reserved. Except for brief quotations in critical publications or reviews, no part of this book may be reproduced in any manner without prior written permission from the publisher. Write: Permissions, Wipf and Stock Publishers, 199 W. 8th Ave., Suite 3, Eugene, OR 97401.

Wipf & Stock
An Imprint of Wipf and Stock Publishers
199 W. 8th Ave., Suite 3
Eugene, OR 97401

www.wipfandstock.com

PAPERBACK ISBN: 978-1-6667-0254-5
HARDCOVER ISBN: 978-1-6667-0255-2
EBOOK ISBN: 978-1-6667-0256-9

03/11/21

Dedicated to my loving wife of 48 years, my family, and my many friends.

Contents

Introduction | 1
Background | 6
Creation | 10
Application | 12
Abraham | 13
Jacob | 17
Moses | 19
Samuel | 23
David | 25
Nathan | 28
Isaiah | 30
Ezekiel | 32
Daniel | 35
Elijah | 38
Jeremiah | 44
Joseph (the Father of Jesus) | 47
John the Baptist | 49
Peter the Apostle | 52
Paul the Apostle | 74
John the Apostle | 76
James the Apostle | 89
Mary Magdalene | 91
Birth of Jesus | 95
Testing of Jesus | 97

Garden of Gethsemane | 99
Death of Jesus | 101
Resurrection of Jesus | 103
The Rapture | 105
Tribulation | 107
The Second Coming | 108
Revelation | 111
Messenger of Evil | 112
Message of Love for Mankind | 114
Message of Spiritual Joy | 116
Message of God's Gift of His Son | 121
Message of Longsuffering | 128
Message of Kindness | 135
Message of Self Control | 140
Message of the Law | 145
Conclusion | 150

Bibliography | 165

Introduction

We worship the one and only almighty God. He is the all powerful, knowing, loving, and all wise Creator. We as believers rest and take comfort in the wisdom in the providence of our Father in heaven. He took Saul a man who had devoted his life to the persecution of Christians and transformed him into a man named Paul, a great Apostle of Jesus Christ. Hatred is an extremely powerful emotion within each man that temporarily blinds a person of love and affection. Saul was consumed by anger and hatred and was causing great harm to the early Christian church. However, nothing is impossible for our Lord and Savior. He can transform any man consumed by hate to a God-loving, God-centered man like the Apostle Paul.

God's love is without limits and is available to all mankind. God's gift of eternal life is available to all who believe in the one true Almighty God and the sacrifice He made with the death of His Son for the forgiveness of all of man's sins.

We were all created by the one, true and Almighty God. Our God is a jealous God who will not tolerate any worship by his people of any other god. Any worship by his people of any other god will result in punishment that will be endured to the third and fourth generation. The worship of another god would include the worship of idols or the worship of any other thing (e.g. money) that would prevent you from worshiping the one and true Almighty God.

God communicates with man in a number of different ways throughout each day. One of the most frequent ways God speaks to man is in a still small voice as He whispers a message into the hearts of men. He may speak to us in a dream that you are able to remember the next day or he may speak to us through others. It is not uncommon for God to communicate to us in a conversation with others, hearing a song, reading a book, or recalling a scripture verse.

God's Messengers

Angels were created by God as spiritual beings for the purpose of worshiping God, acting as messengers, following His commands, and protecting all of His creation. Angels are servants of God and should not be worshiped in any way and at any time.

God created countless numbers of angels before the formation of the heavens and earth for the sole purpose of worshiping God and fulfilling His desires. Job 38:6–7 reads, "Whereupon are the foundations thereof fastened? Or who laid the corner stone thereof; When the morning stars sang together, and all the sons of God shouted for Joy?" Angels shouted with joy as they witnessed God creating the earth and the universe. Even though angels are spiritual beings and normally cannot be seen they still have the ability to be to seen and appear as men. Just to name a few sightings; angels did appear at Jesus' grave, they appeared to the shepherds in the field at Jesus' birth, and they appeared to Abraham as men near to his tent. God created angels as eternal beings that carry with them the wisdom of the ages.

There are angels that are assigned for the purpose of protecting each of us through our daily lives. Psalm 91:11 reads, "For he shall give his angels charge over thee, to keep thee in all thy ways." Angels provide protection from physical harm and will give believers the strength to accomplish difficult tasks when walking in God's will. An angel following God's commands released Peter from his chains; unlocked irons gates and lead him to escape his heavily guarded prison cell.

Angels also vary in appearance, size, strength, and may be assigned to specific responsibilities. For example, angels are assigned to each child for their protection. There are also archangels that are higher in status as Michael the Archangel who is assigned as the protector of Israel. It is believed another Archangel is Gabriel who has been responsible for delivering important messages.

Luke 1:26–28 reads, "And in the sixth month the angel Gabriel was sent from God unto a city of Galilee, named Nazareth. To a virgin espoused to a man whose name was Joseph, of the house of David; and the virgin's name was Mary. And the angel came in unto her, and said. Hail, thou that art highly favored, the Lord is with thee: blessed art thou among women."

There is little detailed information about the angels and their specific duties and actions that they take on a daily basis protecting the believers. They are powerful spiritual beings that are able to carry out God's directions. Angels are able to express emotions with rejoicing in their worshiping God.

Introduction

Our focus is to pray each day for God's direction and allowed our minds and souls to be open to His direction.

Lucifer was a beautiful and powerful angel that rebelled against God. He was known as the light bearer because he was one of the brightest lights in Heaven.

Ezekiel 28:17 reads, "Thine heart was lifted up because of thy beauty, thou hast corrupted thy wisdom by reason of thy brightness: I will cast thee to the ground, I will lay thee before kings, that they may behold thee."

Lucifer became proud because of his beauty and his pride lead to his rebellion. His free will allowed him to choose sin and lead many more angels into sin with him.

Revelations 12:7-9 reads, "And there was war in heaven: Michael and his angels fought against the dragon; and the dragon fought and his angels, And prevailed not; neither was their place found any more in heaven. And the great dragon was cast out, that old serpent, called the Devil, and Satan, which deceiveth the whole world: he was cast out into the earth, and his angels were cast out with him."

Satan is certainly the god of this world and he and his fallen angels have a major hold on what men do and think. However, Satan cannot move without God's permission and he must have God's permission before placing any undue pressure on any one man. Man's biggest weaknesses are related to pride, ego, materialism, money, and lusts. Satan's sin of pride and the resulting rebellion against God is the same sin that men struggle with today. God may allow Satan and his fallen angels to test man for the purposes of strengthening him as a believer. God may use trials and temptations to increase mans' understanding of his weaknesses, to develop positive behaviors traits, to strengthen his ability to say no to temptations, and to address new challenges with the truth. Satan is able to prevent a man from thinking clearly and seeing the blessings from living a Christ-centered life. Many men of today are focused entirely on self and are consumed by Satan's pride. The idea of letting go and placing all of your trust in God to control your life seems impossible to the man of today. The truth is that simply praying for God to enter your life and asking for the forgiveness of your sins is all that is required to spend eternity in heaven with God.

Unfortunately, both Adam and his wife Eve fell victim to Satan's persuasions and sinned against God. The result has been that all of mankind since that time has been subject to and struggled with the fallen nature of sin. The Apostle Paul struggled with sin and realized that he was a carnal man and that he was completely depended on Jesus Christ for salvation.

Romans 7:14–18 reads, "For we know that the law is spiritual: but I am carnal, sold under sin. For that which I do I allow not: for what I would, that do I not; but what I hate, that do I. If then I do that which I would not, I consent unto the law that it is good. Now then it is no more I that do it, but sin that dwelleth in me. For I know that in me (that is, in my flesh,) dwelleth no good thing: for to will is present with me; but how to perform that which is good I find not."

The Apostle Paul and all of mankind are under the influence of Satan and are only able to break free from Satan's grasp with a complete surrender to living a life committed to Jesus Christ.

Today man lives in a world that is influenced by Satan and his demons in many different ways. His strategy is to deceive people into believing his lies, divide people into becoming enemies, and to destroy people by creating ideas and opinions that leads to hate and death. Man has many weaknesses (e.g. pride, greed, lust) that can be easily used by Satan to confuse man into believing that he has experienced some type of disrespect, been lied to, or cheated out of what rightful belongs to him.

Today man is living in a world that is in the middle of a battle between Satan (evil) and God (love). Man is required to make daily decisions to follow God and His commandments or Satan and his deceptive lies. One of Satan's common lies today is that God wants man to accumulate great wealth and live in a mansion. The truth is that God asked the rich young ruler to give all his wealth away and follow him. The truth is that God wants all men to open their hearts and ask for the forgiveness of all their sins and receive God's Holy Spirit. The Holy Spirit will come into a person's life and live with them and direct their paths. Man's primary purpose in this life is to follow God's will for their lives.

The Holy Spirit is part of the Trinity and has always existed as part of the Eternal Almighty God. The Holy Spirit lives within a Christian and provides spiritual growth, wisdom, conviction, transformation, inspiration, and protection. A Christian's seal of salvation is completed by the Holy Spirit as a Christian is reconciled to God for eternity.

Angels were created by God as Spirits that exist for the purpose of serving and glorifying God. God has used angels in a number of different ways to carry out His will from the time of creation until today. Angels have acted as messengers, protectors, and comforters throughout the Old and

Introduction

New Testament. They have the ability to communicate with us through our thoughts, emotions, and impressions. They are concerned about explaining miracles and other issues that are difficult for us to understand and may make us fearful.

Background

A CHRISTIAN BELIEVES THAT the Holy Bible is the inerrant word of God. They believe in God the Father, God the Son, and God the Holy Spirit. They believe that God sent His only Son to die on the cross for all of man's sins. A Christian has prayed for the forgiveness of all his sins and asked God to take control of his life. They believe there will be a judgment day where man will be held accountable for all of his sins. Those who have made a decision to become a Christian and have turned control of their life over to God will be allowed to enter heaven.

Man is in a fallen state due to the sins and decisions made by Adam and Eve in the Garden of Eden. Their decision to listen to Satan and their pride of life has had a profound effect on man's relationship with God. Since that time man has been forced to till the land and work hard to provide enough food to survive the seasons, disease, and physical weakness. Tilling the ground to produce food is difficult work and will be accompanied by some weeds and thorns. Raising a family has always been difficult and requires our continual attention to pull out the weeds and thorns that have been planted by Satan. Women have been forced to endure the pain of child birth and work hard to provide food and clothing for the family. God has continued to allow man to use his free will in making decisions. Consequently, this relationship has been dependent on man's willingness to obey God's commandments, worship, and thank him for his many blessings.

A person who has made the decision to become a Christian will have the opportunity to grow, be blessed by God and have angels surround them for the remainder of their life. Although we may not see them they are around us under God's direction as we travel through our lives. Angels are actively involved in a Christian's life by providing for specific needs that are determined by God. Hebrews 1:14 reads, "Are they not all ministering spirits, sent forth to minister for them who shall be heirs of salvation?" Angels are sent by God to encourage, strengthen, and protect the Christian with God's blessings. Once we make that decision to become a Christian we are under the watchful eye of many angels that can respond in any number of different ways and in any number of different situations under God's direction. Angels are also messengers from God that can communicate messages of comfort, peace, love, warning, and judgment.

Angels are also greatly involved in the daily lives of men and will show great joy when a sinner is found and returned to the community of believers.

Luke 15:7 reads, "I say unto you, that likewise joy shall be in heaven over one sinner that repenteth, more than over ninety and nine just persons, which need no repentance."

God's focus is on the sinner and bringing him to the saving grace and knowledge and belief in Jesus the Christ.

The Apostle Paul also provides instruction on the importance of the Holy Spirit and how he makes it possible for God to hear our prayers.

Romans 8:26 reads, "Likewise the Spirit also helpeth our infirmities: for we know not what we should pray for as we ought: but the Spirit itself maketh intercessions for us with groaning which cannot be uttered."

The Holy Spirit is able to communicate with the Trinity in ways that is not available to man.

The believer has a great deal of resources available to him with the Holy Spirit that lives within him and the angels that are waiting to serve him with the delivery of messages, carry out God's direction and provide comfort if needed. Prayer is extremely important due to the fact it allows the Holy Spirit to open communications with God the Father to relay the believers every request. Without prayer the Holy Spirit is compromised and God's angels are not used. A Christian who has a powerful prayer life will have a group of angels around him to meet his needs and a Spirit and Soul that will be sealed with the Holy Spirit.

When Jesus returns he will judge all of mankind. Each and every Christian's name will also be listed in the book of life. This book lists the name of every person that has turned from rebellion against God and has placed their complete trust in God and has asked for the forgiveness of all of their sins in complete humility. Satan and all of his demons will be casted into the lake of fire for all of eternity.

Revelation 20:15 reads, "And whosoever was not found written in the book of life was cast into the lake of fire."

The Apostle Paul wrote in I Thessalonians 4:13–18, "But I would not have you to be ignorant, brethren, concerning them which are asleep, that ye sorrow not, even as others which have no hope. For if we believe that Jesus died and rose again, even so them also which sleep in Jesus will God bring with him. For this we say unto you by the word of the Lord, that we which are alive and remain unto the coming of the Lord shall not prevent them which are asleep."

The Apostle Paul explains that Jesus will bring with Him at the final judgment all the Christians that have died in the past.

2 Corinthians 5:6–7 reads, "Therefore we are always confident, knowing that, whilst we are at home in the body, we are absent from the Lord: (For we walk by faith, not by sight:)"

The Apostle Paul explains in these verses that Christians are either serving the Lord in this life or serving the Lord in heaven. When a Christian dies they go directly to heaven and wait for the final judgment.

Luke 23:42–43 reads, "And he said unto Jesus, Lord, remember me when thou comest into thy kingdom. And Jesus said unto him, Verily I say unto thee, Today shalt thou be with me in paradise."

The thief while hanging on the cross pleaded with Jesus to have mercy on his soul. The thief realized that his soul would live on after his death and that he needed to be prepared for judgment. Jesus explained that those who have true faith and ask for forgiveness will go immediately into heaven after their bodies die.

Each Christian is unique and each Christian follows a unique path prepared for him by God. In addition, each Christian's life is composed of works that are either Christ centered or self centered. Some Christians are involved in more sin than other Christians. Consequently, we all must appear before the judgment seat of Jesus Christ.

2 Corinthians 5:10 reads, "For we must all appear before the judgment seat of Christ; that every one may receive the things done in his body, according to that he hath done, whether it be good or bad."

1 Corinthians 3:13–14 reads, "Every man's work shall be made manifest: for the day shall declare it, because it shall be revealed by fire; and the fire shall try every man's work of what sort it is. If any man's work abide which he hath built thereupon, he shall receive a reward."

We will all stand before the judgment seat and account for what we have done with our lives. Have we been faithful to our Lord and Savior and followed His commandments? Were we concerned about the lost and worked to make a difference in other's lives? Did we use our blessings from God to make a difference in other people's lives? Did we pray for others and ask God for direction?

Daniel 12:3 reads, "And they that be wise shall shine as the brightness of the firmament; and they that turn many to righteousness as the stars forever and ever."

A Christian will shine as a bright light in heaven for the works that were completed on earth. Those Christians that have turned many to righteousness will shine as stars forever.

Creation

THE CREATION OF THE earth and the entire universe was created by God under His direction and according to His timetable. It is believed that angels too numerous to count shouted with joy as they witnessed God's creation unfold before them.

Job 38:7 reads, "When the morning stars sang together, and all the sons of God shouted for joy?"

It was God's angelic beings (the morning stars and sons of God) and all of God's ministering spirits that shouted with joy as they experienced God's majesty, almighty power and loving grace in the unfolding of creation.

Psalm 148: 1–3 reads, "Praise ye the Lord: Praise ye the Lord from the heavens: praise him in the heights. Praise ye him, all his angels: praise ye him, all his hosts. Praise ye him, sun and moon: praise him, all ye stars of light."

Only the Sovereign and Omnipotent God is able to explain and answer the many questions related to creation.

God created man in His own image with the ability to experience great joy and great sorrow, and is capable of great evil and great good. It isn't until a man realizes he needs to place all of his trust in God for direction and prays for the salvation of his soul that the Holy Spirit enters his life. At this point man experiences great joy that fills his soul and spirit and allows for the communion of man's soul with man's creator, God. The vast crevasse that was created between heaven and a fallen world when man sinned may be crossed with a prayer made in complete humility asking for forgiveness and submitting to God's commandments.

Isaiah 59:2 reads, "But your iniquities have separated between you and your God, and your sins have hid his face from you, that he will not hear."

Ezekiel 14:5 reads, "That I may take the house of Israel in their own heart, because they are all estranged from me through their idols."

CREATION

The idols of today are present everywhere and are being promoted by many as a path to success and a joy filled life. The joy that is realized from the purchase of these idols is generally short lived and is a bad investment. Anything that separates or prevents you from worshiping God in any way is an idol.

God created the angels as spiritual beings with free will and the ability to appear as humans. Their purpose is to worship God, protect and guide God's believers, and to ensure God's will is completed. Angels are present in the believer's daily life on a spiritual level as they communicate with the soul, spirit, heart and mind. Angels will also battle with evil spirits as they try to direct men from entertaining evil thoughts, engaging in evil acts, and doing harm to their fellow man.

God's angels are focused on carrying out God's commandments.

Acts 7:52–53 reads, "Which of the prophets have not your fathers persecuted? and they have slain them which showed before of the coming of the Just One; of whom ye have been now the betrayers and murderers: Who have received the law by the disposition of angels, and have not kept it."

Deuteronomy 33:2 reads, "And he said, The Lord came from Sinai, and rose up from up from Seir unto them; he shined forth from mount Paran, and he came with ten thousands of saints: from his right hand went a fiery law for them."

Angels were present with God when he appeared to Moses on Mount Sinai.

God created the heavens and the earth and all those things that are present. He also created all those things that are not seen. The fact that we do not see something does not mean it does not exist. For example, we do not see disease, gravity, air, sound, many dangerous gases, and dangerous rays from the sun, etc. Realizing our limited ability to see many things it is not unreasonable to think that there are many more things we do not see on a daily basis. An angel could be standing in front of us without our seeing the angel or hearing its message. It is only with God grace that those who have humbled themselves before the Lord and have open their hearts that are able to hear the message.

God created angels for a number of different reasons and are present as spiritual beings in different forms and shapes. They fill different purposes and fall into different hierarchies. Generally, when angels do appear they will warn people not to be afraid. They realize most people will be terrified and panic when seeing an angel.

Application

God has created millions of millions of angels for the purpose of praising God and protecting His creation, man. As soon as man accepts the fact that God has sent His only Son to die on the Cross for all of man's sin he opens the door to all of God's blessings. Many of these blessings in many ways are delivered by angels to man. A man's daily life may involve many angels that are providing communication, protection, and direction.

Psalm 34:7 reads, "The angel of the Lord encampeth around about them that fear him, and delivereth them."

Psalm 91:11 reads, "For he shall give his angels charge over thee, to keep thee in all thy ways."

There is a spiritual war that surrounds us each day. For the Christian, God has sent His angels to protect us from Satan and all of evil ways. Satan and his evil demons attack man each day in many different ways and from many different sources. It is God's angels that block or eliminate many of these dangers. Some of God's angels are extremely powerful and have the ability to remove any insurmountable road block or challenges.

However, we live in a fallen world that is full of dangers and we need to be prepared. We all will encounter some disappointments, sorrow, and pain. God will use some of these difficulties to teach us, mold us, and make us into people that are kind, understanding, and compassionate.

It is hard to believe that millions of people have rejected Christianity.

Abraham

Approximately (2166 BC to 1991 BC)

THREE ANGELS APPEARED AS three men before Abraham at his tent in the plains of Mamre. Abraham recognized who they were and ran to meet them and bowed himself before them. Others that saw these three men did not recognize they were spiritual beings. The angel of God spoke to Abraham directly and explained to him that even though Sarah was old she would give birth to a son.

The angel of God and two other Angels in this situation appeared as humans. They appeared to Abraham for the purpose of delivering a message about Sarah giving birth and the destruction of Sodom and Gomorrah. Abraham tried to negotiate with God about the destruction of Sodom and Gomorrah by pointing out that there were a number of righteous people living in the cities. Unfortunately, there were no righteous people living in the cities other than Lot and his family. The two angels traveled to Lot's home where they were attacked by a group of men. In this situation God directed the two angels to blind the attackers and provide protection for the removal of Lot and his family.

Genesis 19:15 reads, "And when the morning arose, then the angels hastened Lot, saying, Arise take thy wife, and thy two daughters, which are here; lest thou be consumed in the iniquity of the city."

The spiritual battle that was present in Sodom and Gomorrah is still going on today. Satan is still revolting against the all powerful God. However, today we do not see the spiritual battle that is raging around us. Most people are overwhelmed by the realities of today's world and live in state of confusion created by Satan's many lies.

Ephesians 6:12 reads, "For we wrestle not against flesh and blood, but against principalities, against powers, against the rulers of the darkness of this world, against spiritual wickedness in high places."

The lives that we live out daily are in many ways influenced and determined in many respects by the decisions we make throughout our lives. Many of these decisions that are made are subject to Satan's influences and can have a devastating impact throughout our entire lives. The importance of prayer cannot be minimized and must be petitioned to God each day. Those individuals that decide to become Christians will experience the indwelling of God's Holy Spirit and will be given access to His direction. A Christian realizes that God has a plan for their lives and that plan will include using the gifts and talents that were given to them by God. The Christian will also experience the peace of God which cannot be explained in human terms.

Philippians 4:7 reads, "And the peace of God, which passeth all understanding, shall keep your hearts and minds through Christ Jesus."

Application

Angels are able to take on the human form, eat food and take on any number of other human characteristic. They also have free will and are able to rebel against God. Most men are not able to recognize an angel in their human form. Abraham and Lot were able to recognize these visitors as angels due to their relationship with God. Therefore, they followed the angel's instructions and were able to escape from Sodom and Gomorrah.

Other men in Sodom and Gomorrah did not realize who these strangers were because of the sin in their lives. Sin will infest a man's heart and soul to the point of blocking a man from seeing, hearing and realizing God's purpose for his life. We are in the middle of an ongoing spiritual war between good and evil. Angels are with us each day as we struggle in this spiritual war.

Today, there is an ongoing controversy as to whether man can see angels. It is generally believed, that man would be terrified if he were to see an angel in it's natural state and then would be placed in the difficult position of explaining what they saw. However, we also know that Mary Magdalene mistook Jesus as a gardener at Jesus' grave.

John 20:15 reads, "Jesus saith unto her, Women, why weepest thou whom seekest thou? She, supposing him to be the gardener, saith unto him,

Sir, if thou have borne him hence, tell me where thou hast laid him, and I will take him away."

The curtain that separates us from heaven is impossible for us to see through, but at the same time it is only a moment away from where we are. Jesus and his angels are able to cross from the physical to the spiritual with ease. Throughout history God has used angels to deliver important messages to his people. In some cases, angels that were selected to deliver these messages took on the form of a human. In many cases, those angels that have appeared began a message by saying "fear not." Obviously, in some cases an angel's appearance can be terrifying to some and is in need of some type of introduction that would warn a person of a possible difficult and disturbing sight. This warning may allow a person some time to quiet their souls and spirits to be open to hearing a message of importance.

Again, we know that God created millions of angels as eternal, spiritual beings capable of appearing to man if needed in different forms. There are also angels that sing praises to God and rejoice greatly as each new person comes to the knowledge of the saving grace of their Savior and Lord. Our knowledge of God and His angels is extremely limited and may not be available for human explanation in great detail.

Angels are mentioned throughout the Bible from Genesis to Revelations praising God, protecting, encouraging, comforting believers, and communicating messages to God and delivering messages from God. Obviously, angels have always been available to God for carrying out His Will and purpose in the believer's life.

Revelation 5:11–12 reads, "And I beheld, and I heard the voice of many angels round about the throne and the beasts and the elders: and the number of them was ten thousand times ten thousand, and thousands of thousands; Saying with a loud voice, Worthy is the Lamb that was slain to receive power, and riches, and wisdom, and strength, and honor, and glory, and blessing."

A myriad (too many to count) of angels were created by God for His will and purpose. God is the same today and forever. God never changes and He will continue to use His angels as messengers to deliver His will and purpose for the believer's life. We may not see these angels, but they continue to protect us in many ways and deliver messages to the believer's soul, mind, and spirit through dreams, songs, prayers, Bible study, and other ways. We may in fact be in a room with hundreds of angels and not aware of their presence. They have the wisdom of the ages and may simply bear witness to our successes and failures. They may be simply waiting for God's command to send a message, provide protection, or intervene in some way.

Abraham was able to see that the men that appeared in front of his tent were angels. If these men were to appear before us today would we be able to determine if they were angels? Does any man today have the same close relationship Abraham had with God? God is the same today, yesterday, and forever.

Jacob

Approximately (1836 BC to 1689 BC)

JACOB THE SON OF Isaac and Rebecca had a number of experiences with angels over his life of 147 years. Jacob's first encounter with angels was in a dream where he saw a stairway that started on earth and reached to heaven.

Genesis 28:12 reads, "And he dreamed, and behold a ladder set up on the earth, and top of it reached to heaven: and behold the angels of God ascending and descending on it."

The dream of these angels continually moving to and from heaven illustrates how God was continually with Jacob and how God's angels were continually delivering messages, blessings, and carrying out His will and plan for all of mankind.

Jacob had another dream where an angel called out to Jacob.

Genesis 31:11 reads, "And the angel of God spake unto me in a dream, saying, Jacob: And I said, Here am I."

Here is another example of an angel delivering a message from God to Jacob. In this situation, God wants to get Jacob's attention and for him to start to plan for his move back to his own land, Canaan, the land of promise.

Application

In this situation, angels appeared to Jacob in a dream and provided some type of explanation as to how angels move from heaven to earth and back. In some respects a dream is the perfect method for God himself or an angel to communicate a message since the person dreaming is normally relaxed and is open to new ideas and suggestions.

God's Messengers

God is the same today, yesterday and forever. God has revealed himself in dreams to man throughout history.

1 Kings 3:5 reads, "In Gibeon the Lord appeared to Solomon in a dream by night: and God said, Ask what I shall give thee."

This dream was extremely important because Solomon's answer in the dream pleased God and sealed the faith of all those that would experience Solomon's judgments.

1Kings 3:12 reads, "Behold, I have done according to thy words: lo, I have given thee a wise and an understanding heart; so that there was none like thee before thee, neither after thee shall any arise like unto thee."

This dream was created by God for the purpose of getting Solomon's attention and getting him to think about what was important in his life. Solomon's answer pleased God and resulted in Solomon receiving a blessing beyond measure. No man has ever been as wise as Solomon.

Another example of God using dreams was when God spoke to Joseph.

Matthew 1:20 reads, "But while he thought on these things, behold, the angel of the Lord appeared unto him in a dream, saying, Joseph, thou son of David, fear not to take unto thee Mary thy wife: for that which is conceived in her is of the Holy Ghost."

Joseph was greatly perplexed and under extremely pressure to find a solution that would resolve many social and religious problems. A dream was the perfect method by placing Joseph in a deep sleep that allowed God to communicate to Joseph a complicated and hard to believe message. Joseph had to disregard all that he understood of conception and place all of his faith in God's plan.

Most of the dreams we have on a daily basis have no meaning and in some cases are simply a review of past experiences. However, God may use a dream as a way to communicate a message to us. It is possible for God to use a dream to warn us of an impending danger, provide guidance in making a decision, or bring to light a forgotten fact. God's messages are endless and include endless possibilities.

Moses

Approximately (1391 BC to 1271 BC)

GOD SENT HIS ANGEL to Moses and the Israelites to protect and guide them as they traveled through the wilderness after escaping from Egypt and the Pharaoh.

Exodus 23:20-22 reads, "Behold, I send an angel before thee, to keep thee in the way, and to bring thee into the place which I have prepared. Beware of him, and obey his voice, provoke him not; for he will not pardon your transgressions: for my name is in him. But if thou shalt indeed obey his voice, and do all that I speak; then I will be an enemy unto thine enemies, and an adversary unto thine adversaries."

God warns Moses not to provoke this angel in any way, but to simply obey him as he provides directions. This angel speaks directly to Moses with God's authority and expects Moses to act without question and follow his directions to the letter. In this case there is no room for discussion or for any type of compromise.

God knew Moses and his weaknesses. When God first spoke to Moses in Midian he lacked many character traits that would make him a great leader. Moses said he wasn't good enough to lead the Israelites, he wasn't an eloquent speaker, and he wasn't qualified. God met Moses where he was and gave Moses the knowledge and character traits needed to be successful. Moses learned that he needed to trust God for the strength and wisdom and to move forward and stop making excuses. If you depend on God for your strength and wisdom he will direct his angels to protect you in many ways.

Psalm 91:9-12 reads. "Because thou hast made the Lord, which is my refuge, even the most high, thy habitation; There shall no evil befall thee, neither shall any plague come nigh thy dwelling. For he shall give his angels charge over thee, to keep thee in all thy ways. They shall bear thee up in their hands, lest thou dash thy foot against a stone."

The Lord came to Moses with thousands of angels in preparing the law at Sinai.

Psalm 68:17 reads, "The chariots of God are twenty thousand, even thousands of angels: the Lord is among them, as in Sinai, in the holy place."

Deuteronomy 33:1–3 reads, "And this is the blessing, wherewith Moses the man of God blessed the children of Israel before his death. And he said, The Lord came from Sinai, and rose up from Seir unto them; he shined forth from mount Paran, and he came with ten thousands of saints: from his right hand went a fiery law for them. Yea, he loved the people; all his saints are in thy hand: and they sat down at thy feet; everyone shall receive of thy words."

Angels are God's messengers and often accompany Him during important events. The angels that accompany God are powerful and holy. They saw the fall of Satan, the fall of man, and God's judgment and punishment. They understand and love the scriptures and righteousness.

Application

God created man out of His love and grace and made it possible for all to spend eternity with Him. It is estimated that 100 billion people have lived on this world with over seven billion living today. However, it was God's sacrifice that made it possible for the sins for these billions of people to be forgiven with a decision to believe in God and the sacrifice of His Son. God sacrificed His only Son and raised Him after three days to overcome death and the power of Satan. The scope and wonder of this miracle is beyond our comprehension. Only one person was able to live his life on this world without sin and that was God's Son, Jesus Christ. Man's faith and love for the One True Almighty God and His Son opens the door for salvation for all of mankind. Today, we are still in the middle of a war between good and evil. God has deployed His many angels that are continually protecting us from Satan and his many demons. In most cases, we do not know of these attacks or understand how they are affecting our daily lives.

Ephesians 6:12 reads, "For we wrestle not against flesh and blood, but against principalities, against powers, against the rulers of the darkness of this world, against spiritual wickedness in high places."

Satan is the great liar, deceiver, who is looking at every opportunity to rob man of God's blessings. The major objective of Satan is for man to destroy himself. He uses man's weaknesses (i.e., pride, lust, greed) to create a situation where man is at war with each other over positions and status. Man in his fallen state is easily convinced by Satan to act according to his wishes. As stated before, Satan is trying to convince man to destroy himself by any means possible.

Moses spoke directly to God and at times with angels. God spoke directly to Moses and told him he and his brother Aaron would need to approach Pharaoh to ask for the release of the Israelites. God spoke directly to Moses ten times giving him and Aaron directions as to how the ten plagues would unfold and how they would impact Pharaoh and the people of Egypt. Moses was about 80 years of age and Aaron was about 83 during this time. Moses died at the age of 120 and Aaron at 123 after wandering for 40 years in the desert. During these 40 years God spoke directly to Moses as a friend and gave Moses instruction as how to direct and lead the Israelites during this difficult journey.

It is believed that the Angel of the Lord is a special angel that God uses in special situations to deliver important messages. The Angel of the Lord spoke directly to Moses to ensure the release of the Israelites from Egypt and the Pharaoh. The release of the Israelites from Egypt would require God's power and wisdom to make the Pharaoh give up an extremely valuable asset to Egypt. The Israelites represented a major portion of Egypt's slave labor force and were responsible for building many the Pharaoh's massive structures.

The other angel that is mentioned is the destroyer (angel of death) that will visit those homes without the blood of a lamb posted on their doors.

Exodus 12: 23 reads, "For the Lord will pass through to smite the Egyptians; and when he seeth the blood upon the lintel, and on the two side posts, the Lord will pass over the door, and will not suffer the destroyer to come in unto your houses to smite you."

The Israelites were required to sacrifice a lamb without blemishes and place the blood from the lamb on the top door support and on the two sides of the door to protect their first born from the angel of death.

God sent His angel to go ahead of the Israelites to provide protection and direction as they traveled through the wildness to the Promised Land of Canaan. We need to accept God's gift of protection and trust in His angels directions.

Hebrew 1:14 reads, " Are they not all ministering spirits, sent forth to minister for them who shall be heirs of salvation."

Angels work for God in providing protection for the believer. Angels assist the believer in many different ways in avoiding sin on their path to eternal life. The angel is able to communicate to God in all possible situations. The decision made by the believer to accept God's invitation for salvation allows angels to minister to the believer in many different ways. As believers we are protected by angels on a daily basis as we follow God's purpose and will for our life.

This angel of the covenant was an angel of great power that could destroy many armies and could bring great fear to anyone that would dare to resist. God tells Moses and Aaron to obey this angel's commands and do not provoke him with any resistance. This angel has God's name within him and represents God's direction.

Jeremiah prophesied (640BC-586BC) that a new covenant would confirm the blessings of the old and the unchangeable laws of God. Under the new covenant God's law would be written on the hearts of man where God's love may be experienced within all man.

Jeremiah 31:31-34 reads, "Behold, the days come," saith the Lord, "that I will make a new covenant with the house of Israel, and with the house of Judah. Not according to the covenant that I made with their fathers in the day that I took them by the hand to bring them out of the land of Egypt; which my covenant they brake, although I was a husband unto them, saith the lord: But this shall be the covenant that I will make with the house of Israel; After those days, saith the Lord, I will put my law in their inward parts, and write it in their hearts; and will be their God, and they shall be my people. And they shall teach no more every man his neighbor, and every man his brother, saying, Know the Lord: for they shall all know me, from the least of them unto the greatest of them, saith the Lord: for I will forgive their iniquity, and I will remember their sin no more."

The Israelites had failed during their bondage in Egypt and failed to keep God's law in the wilderness. Christ announced in the upper room that a new covenant would be sealed with His blood on the cross. The new covenant allowed the Holy Spirit to enter into a man's spirit and provide moral direction and a realization of Gods' mercy and grace. The new covenant was the gift of God's only Son Jesus the Savior of all mankind. The forgiveness of all of man's sin was only possible with the sacrifice of God's greatest gift the death of His only Son on the cross.

Samuel

Approximately (1070BC to 1012BC)

SAMUEL'S LIFE BEGAN AS an answer to prayer. Hannah his mother had prayed for many years before giving birth to Samuel. At an early age, Samuel was placed under the religious training of Eli a leader and high priest.

1 Samuel 3:16 -17 reads, "Then Eli called Samuel, and said, Samuel, my son. And he answered, Here am I. And he said, What is the thing that the Lord hath said unto thee? I pray thee hide it not from me: God do so to thee, and more also, if thou hide any thing from me of all the things that he said unto thee."

Eli realized Samuel had a special relationship with God and that God was providing Samuel with important information. Samuel grew in his relationship with God and faithfully provided God's messages to the people of Israel. Samuel loved God and obeyed Him without question. It was this type of commitment that created within him unquestionable integrity.

God used Samuel to communicate His messages in many ways. Samuel anointed both King Saul and King David thereby moving Israel's leadership from Judges to Kings.

1 Samuel 15:10–11 reads, "Then came the word of the Lord unto Samuel, saying, It repenteth me that I have set up Saul to be King: for he is turned back from following me, and hath not performed my commandments. And it grieved Samuel; and he cried unto the Lord all night."

Again, God speaks directly to Samuel and tells Samuel that He regrets setting up Saul as King because of his disobedience.

1 Samuel 16:1 reads, "And the Lord said unto Samuel, How long wilt thou mourn for Saul, seeing I have rejested him from reigning over Israel? Fill thine horn with oil, and go, I will send thee to Jesse the Bethlehemite: for I have provided me a king among his sons."

1 Samuel 16:10–13 reads, "Again, Jesse made seven of his sons to pass before Samuel. And Samuel said unto Jesse, The Lord hath not chosen these. And Samuel said unto Jesse, Are here all thy children? And he said, There remaineth yet the youngest, and, behold, he keepeth the sheep. And Samuel said unto Jesse, Send and fetch him: for we will not sit down till he come hither. And he sent, and brought him in. Now he was ruddy, and withal of a beautiful countenance, and goodly to look to. And the Lord said, Arise, anoint him: for this is he. Then Samuel took the horn of oil, and anointed him in the midst of his brethren: and the Spirit of the Lord came upon David from that day forward. So Samuel rose up, and went to Ramah."

God had selected David not because of his experience, wealth, knowledge, position, or his physical stature. God selected David because of his heart and his willingness to obey God's direction. David loved God with all his heart, soul and mind. He was eager to obey God's commands and lived to please God.

Application

Samuel was throughout his entire life a man who followed the law and placed his trust in God for direction. God used Samuel to anoint kings and to instruct many on how to be obedient to God's word.

God will use those who are obedient to His word and have opened their hearts to His will. Samuel was also a judge who was able to determine justice for many different legal cases.

Samuel was a man who was able to recognize sin in his life and in the life others. The repentance of sin is an important part of a Christian's life and must be exercised throughout a Christian's life. Sin and the failure to recognize sin and not to make changes will block a closer relationship with God. God loves the sinner, but hates the sin. 1 John 3:6 reads, "If we say that we have fellowship with him, and walk in darkness, we lie, and do not the truth."

David

Approximately (1000BC to 970BC)

DAVID WAS A GREAT King because of his great relationship with God. It is generally believed that David was anointed by Samuel to be king very early in his life. Some believe David was only ten to thirteen years of age when anointed to be king by Samuel. However, becoming king would not occur until David reached the age of thirty and endured a great deal of challenges and hardships over many years. Initially, David was accepted by King Saul as a musician and a soldier and was not considered a threat to his reign.

However, Saul eventually learned of David's secret anointment by Samuel and plotted to have David eliminated. Consequently, David spent many years running and hiding in the wilderness in an effort to escape capture by Saul's soldiers.

God was faithful and protected David throughout these many years in the wilderness. During these years, David learned that the first response to any issues was to worship God and ask for His blessings and direction.

1 Kings 14:8 reads, ". . .and yet thou hast not been as my servant David, who kept my commandments, and who followed me with all his heart, to do that only which was right in mine eyes;"

David became a great king, but not without many grueling years of distress and despair. It was only through these many difficult years that David learned how much God loved him and cared for him.

God's love for David came in the form of forgiveness, grace and mercy. David, in turn showed this same love, mercy and forgiveness as King of Israel. David had learned to place his complete trust in God and no longer reacted to attacks about his honor and position. David understood that God was in charge of his life and God would protect him from those who would try to discredit him in any way. In fact, God's response to any injustice or unprovoked action against David was much more severe than anything David could have contrived.

David was also a great warrior that expanded the kingdom and was able to build a huge army that was respected throughout the region. David was able to capture Jerusalem back from the Jebusites and made it into the capital of Israel.

2 Samuel 8:11–15 reads, "Which also king David did dedicate unto the Lord, with the silver and gold that he had dedicated of all the nations which he subdued; Of Syria, and of Moab, and of the children of Ammon, and of th Philistines, and of Amalek, and of the spoil of Hadadezer, son of Rehob, king of Zobah. And David gat him a name when he returned from smiting of the Syrians in the valley of salt, being eighteen thousand men. And he put garrisons in Edom; throughout all Edom put he garrisons, and all they of Edom became David's servants. And the Lord preserved David whithersoever he went. And David reigned over all Israel; and David executed judgment and justice unto all his people."

David with his army was able to bring unification back to the twelve tribes. Israel and Judah once again became one country, Israel. Jerusalem became the location for the Temple of God and the Ark.

Acts 13:22 reads, "And when he had removed him, he raised up unto them David to be their king; to whom also he gave testimony, and said, I have found David the son of Jesse, a man after mine own heart, which shall fulfill all my will."

It was David whom God selected to bring unification back to Israel. Even though David was a sinner, God was able to use him in some powerful ways. David was a man who was humble, God fearing, repentant, and who spent much of his life trying to please God in song, words, and action.

Application

God's messengers to mankind come in many different ways. In this case, God used David to deliver the message as to how God carried out many of His plans for both Israel and mankind.

God selected David to be king of Israel for a number of different reasons. God used David to greatly expand Israel's influence in the region, destroy many enemies, and to consolidate Judah and Israel. However, like most men, David did fail in many different situations and in some cases had to face the consequences for his sin. We are often faced with many difficult situations that at times seem to be insurmountable. Even though David experienced God protection over many years and in many circumstances, he still failed God.

David's humble prayer is one that acknowledges God's greatness and gives thanks for God's many blessings.

2 Samuel 7:18–21 reads, "Then went King David in, and sat before the Lord, and he said, Who am I, O Lord God? and what is my house, that thou hast brought me hitherto? And this was yet a small thing in thy sight, O Lord God; but thou hast spoken also of thy servant's house for a great while to come. And is this the manner of man, O Lord God? And what can David say more unto thee? for thou. Lord God, knowest thy servant. For thy word's sake, and according to thine own heart, hast thou done all these great things, to make thy servant know them."

David begins his pray in complete submission and makes it clear that he is not worthy of God's blessings. David's heart is open waiting to be obedient to God's word.

David was a unique, obedient, highly talented individual that God was able to mold into a great king. David's training was difficult and lasted for many years before God allowed him to be king. This training changed David's perspective as to how he viewed and evaluated different people in different situations. He became more sensitive to others, more compassionate, and gained greater control over his character.

God's love for David and the great accomplishments and the great success of his kingdom paved the way for the bloodline for the Messiah. God's love for mankind is overwhelming and is difficult to comprehend. David's sins were numerous and serious and cannot be minimized in any way. However, like David, we can ask God for the forgiveness for all of our sins and become obedient to His commands.

Nathan

Approximately (1000BC to 900BC)

NATHAN WAS A COURT prophet who lived during the time of King David and King Solomon. He was an advisor to King David and was used by God to deliver a message of rebuke for David's killing of Uriah and the taking of his wife. The consequence of this sin was severe and it resulted in the death of David and Bathsheba's first son.

Psalm 51:1-3 reads, "Have mercy upon me, O God, according to thy lovingkindness: according unto the multitude of thy tender mercies blot out my transgressions. Wash me thoroughly from mine iniquity, and cleanse me from my sin. For I acknowledge my transgressions: and my sin is ever before me."

David was a man who deeply regretted his sin and fell on his face asking God for forgiveness and mercies. David feared he may lose his relationship with God's Holy Spirit and pleaded and begged for days for forgiveness.

David wanted to build God a temple, but God had different plans.

1 Chronicles 17:3-4 reads, "And it came to pass the same night, that the word of God came to Nathan, saying, Go and tell David my servant, Thus saith the Lord, Thou shalt not build me a house to dwell in:"

David hands were responsible for shedding a great deal of blood in battles that brought about peace to Israel. However, God's house needed to be associated with peace, for it was a house of prayer. God would allow the temple to be built by David's son Solomon.

There was some conflict as to who was to replace David as king. Nathan the prophet would again be the messenger for God.

2 Samuel 12:24-25 reads, "And David comforted Bathsheba his wife, and went in unto her, and lay with her: and she bare a son, and called his

name Solomon: and the Lord loved him. And he sent by the hand of Nathan the prophet; and he called his name Jedidiah, because of the Lord."

Nathan the prophet of God was again involved in the life of David in solving issues that seem to occur periodically. God did confirm that Solomon would be the next king regardless of what others said or decided.

Application

Nathan was a messenger of God and served David as a close advisor for many years. Nathan was a prophet and worked in David's court and would convey God's messages to King David.

Today, messages are sent from God to us in many different ways. Many of these messages are revealed to us as ideas or thoughts that may occur during study of God's word, in prayer, or allowing our minds to contemplate possible solutions. In some cases, God will use others to introduce us to new and different ideas. It is important that we do not disregard these ideas simply due to some prejudicial opinion or some unrelated past experience.

God worked with King David as He works with us today. God loved King David because he was a man after God's own heart. Even though David was guilty of many sins he always remained a faithful worshiper of God. David had a passion for God and he asked for forgiveness for all of his sins with great sincerity and humility.

God loves the sinner, but hates the sin. Jesus told the adulterous woman at the well to "go and sin no more." Man was given free will and has the power to sin or not to sin.

James 1:13–15 reads, "Let no man say when he is tempted, I am tempted of God: for God cannot be tempted with evil, neither tempteth he any man: But every man is tempted, when he is drawn away of his own lust, and enticed. Then when lust hath conceived, it bringeth forth sin: and sin, when it is finished, bringeth forth death."

We all live as fallen man and have sins that live inside us. It is our decision to either accept these sinful thoughts and act on them or reject them and take control of our thoughts and actions.

John 14:15 reads, "If ye love me, keep my commandments."

If you love God you will live a life that is based on following God's commandments and showing His love to others.

Isaiah

Approximately (739BC to 681BC)

Isaiah is considered to be one of God's greatest prophets and messengers. He was a Hebrew prophet who lived in Jerusalem about seven hundred years before the birth of Jesus. He foretold the coming of the Messiah and the saving grace for all of man's sins.

Isaiah 40:3-5 reads, "The voice of him that crieth in the wilderness, Prepare ye the way of the Lord, make straight in the desert a highway for our God. Every valley shall be exalter, and every mountain and hill shall be made low: and the crooked shall be made straight, and the rough places plain:"

The people of Judah had turned their backs on God and were involved in worshiping idols and other types of sins. God had condemned the wickedness of the people of Judah and prophesied that they would suffer a severe judgment because of their evil. In many cases these judgments were carried out as other nations were allowed to invade and destroy the land of Israel.

Isaiah 10:10-12 reads, "As my hand hath found the kingdoms of the idols, and whose graven images did excel them of Jerusalem and of Samaria; Shall I not , as I have done unto Samaria and her idols, so do to Jerusalem and her idols?" Wherefore it shall come to pass, that when the Lord hath performed his whole work upon mount Zion and on Jerusalem, I will punish the fruit of the stout heart of the king of Assyria, and the glory of his high look,"

God allowed many nations to invade and destroy the land of Israel because of their failure to remain a righteous people that worship the one true God.

Application

God is the same yesterday, today, and forever. God loved the land of Israel and the people of Israel and disciplined them for their failures. God loves His children and will discipline those whom He loves. God will allow the pain from a fallen world to discipline those whom have failed to live a righteous life.

There is a direct relationship between sin and discipline. There is also a price to be paid for those sins.

Isaiah 2:2–4 reads, "And it shall come to pass in the last days, that the mountain of the Lord's house shall be established in the top of the mountains, and shall be exalted above the hills; and all nations shall flow unto it. And many people shall go and say, come ye, and let us go up to the mountain of the Lord, to the house of the God of Jacob; and he will teach us of his ways, and we will walk in his paths: for out of Zion shall go forth the law, and the word of the Lord from Jerusalem. And he shall judge among the nations, and shall rebuke many people: and they shall beat their swords into plowshares, and their spears into pruninghooks: nation shall not lift up sword against nation, neither shall they learn war any more."

Man is in a fallen state and lives in a fallen world. The only person that lived a sinless life in this world was Jesus Christ. The wages for sin is death and Jesus paid that debt in full on the cross. Jesus bore the wrath of God for all of man's sin so that man would not suffer the price for man's sin. Therefore, 1 John 1:9 reads, "If we confess our sins, he faithful and just to forgive us our sins, and to cleanse us from all unrighteousness."

However, God loves His creation, mankind, and continually works to form mankind into His likeness. The challenges of life will chasten mankind and is designed to bring man into a closer relationship with God. Any unclean though, word, or action will be met with God's discipline.

2 Corinthians 4:17 reads, "For our light affliction, which is but for a moment, worketh for us a far more exceeding and eternal weight of glory; "

Christians live in the hope of things to come. What we see is temporary, but what is unseen, the Spiritual, lives forever.

Ezekiel

Approximately (623 BC to 571 BC)

EZEKIEL WAS A PROPHET and priest from Israel who wrote about the destruction of Jerusalem and the exile of the Israelites to Babylon. At a young age Ezekiel prophesized the judgment of Israel because it trusted in foreign gods and other pagan practices. Ezekiel's prophecies also included hope and the eventual return to Jerusalem and Judah.

Ezekiel 1:1 reads, "Now it came to pass in the thirtieth year, in the fourth month, in the fifth day of the month, as I was among the captives by the river of Chebar, that the heavens were open, and I saw visions of God."

Ezekiel 1:3 reads, "The word of the Lord came expressly unto Ezekiel the priest, the son of Buzi, in the land of the Caldeans by the river Chebar; and the hand of the Lord was there upon him."

Ezekiel's message stressed the importance of worshiping the one true God and that the worship of idols by the people resulted in the exile to Babylon. Ezekiel's prophecy began when he was exiled to Babylon and continued for approximately twenty years.

God spoke through Ezekiel to deliver the message that the worship of idols and other sins was the cause for their exile to Babylon. Ezekiel's prophecy and message was met with rejection and displeasure because he reminded them of their sin.

Ezekiel 2:6 reads, "And thou, son of man, be not afraid of them, neither be afraid of their words, though briers and thorns be with thee, and thou dost dwell among scorpions: be not afraid of their words, not be dismayed at their looks, though they be a rebellious house."

God encouraged Ezekiel not to be afraid and to continue to deliver God's message to those that were exiled. The task was difficult and dangerous and God would provide him with the words to be used. God also provided Ezekiel with additional strength, confidence, and determination.

Ezekiel 34 1–3 reads, "And the word of the Lord came unto me, saying, Son of man, prophesy against the shepherds of Israel, prophesy, and say unto them, Thus saith the Lord God unto the shepherds; Woe be to the shepherds of Israel that do feed themselves! Should not the shepherds feed the flocks? Ye eat the fat, and ye clothe you with the wool, ye kill them that are fed: but ye feed not the flock."

God directs Ezekiel to tell the leaders that God will hold them accountable for not leading the people in a time of need.

Ezekiel 34: 15–16 reads, "I will feed my flock, and I will cause them to lie down, saith the Lord God. I will seek that which was lost, and bring again that which was driven away, and will bind up that which was broken, and will strengthen that which was sick: but I will destroy the fat and the strong; I will feed them with judgment."

God will intervene and rescue His people from Babylon. God will restore Israel and bless His people and land.

Application

God is the same yesterday, today, and forever. Those that were exiled to Babylon with Ezekiel were confused and looking for answers and the reason for their exile. People today are asking the same question that was being asked by God's people in Ezekiel's time. Why me or why is this happening now? God loves His creation and is continually directing them and encouraging them to live a righteous life. God uses the pressures and hardships of this life to bring us to the realization that sin is real and needs to be confessed. We are a work-in-process and God is molding us into his likeness. This process is difficult and requires a real sense of self and the willingness to stop and evaluate your own life

Psalm 137:1–3 reads, "By the rivers of Babylon, there we sat down, yea, we wept, when we remembered Zion. We hanged our harps upon the willows in the midst thereof. For there they that carried us away captive required of us a song; and they that wasted us required of us mirth, saying, Sing us one of the songs of Zion."

As Ezekiel we may be surrounded by scorpions waiting to sting us with their venomous words or actions. However, we serve an all powerful

God who controls both good and evil in this world and has a specific plan for each of us.

2 Corinthians 4:17–18 reads, "For our light affliction, which is but for a moment, worketh for us a far more exceeding and eternal weight of glory; While we look not at the things which are seen: but at the things which are not seen: for the things which are seen are temporal; but the things which are not seen are eternal."

God's love for us has no limits and restrictions. God is focused on our spiritual life and in molding us into a Christ-like person. His goal is to make us into individuals that produce fruit. The master of the vineyard bruins the vines to ensure the plant is healthy and continues to produce fruit. God is at work in our lives using discipline to cut away bad attitudes, unhealthy life practices, and many other sinful distractions that would prevent the production of healthy fruit. God is looking to mold into us Christ-like characteristics and righteousness.

Daniel

Approximately (605 BC to 536 BC)

It is believed that the archangel Gabriel was sent to help Daniel interpret dreams.

Daniel 8:15–18 reads, "And it came to pass, when I, even I Daniel, had seen the vision, and sought for the meaning, then, behold, there stood before me as the appearance of a man. And I heard a man's voice between the banks of Ulai, which called, and said, Gabriel, make this man to understand the vision. So he came near where I stood: and when he came, I was afraid, and fell upon my face: but he said unto me, Understand, O son of man, for at the time of the end shall be the vision. Now as he was speaking with me, I was in a deep sleep on my face toward the ground: but he touched me, and set me upright."

God in this situation sends the archangel Gabriel to communicate to Daniel. It is believed that Gabriel places Daniel in a deep sleep and allowed Daniel access to the spiritual realm.

God also sent His angels to protect Daniel from the lions that were locked in the den with him.

Daniel 6:22 reads, "My God hath sent his angel, and hath shut the lion's mouths, that they have not hurt me: forasmuch as before him innocency was found in me; and also before thee, O King, have I done no hurt."

The angels of God are powerful and capable of controlling wild animals and man. Angels of God are capable of controlling man in many different ways without their knowledge.

God also sent his angels to protect Shadrach, Meshach, and Abednego in the fiery furnace.

Daniel 3:28 reads, "Then Nebuchadnezzar spake, and said, Blessed be the God of Shadrach, Meshach, and Abednego, who hath sent his angel, and delivered his servants that trusted in him, and have changed the king's word, and yielded their bodies, that they might not serve nor worship any god, except their own God."

These three men refused to worship the golden image Nebuchadnezzar had made. God's angel prevented the fire from harming these three men for a number of reasons. God sent his angel to protect these men to show to Nebuchadnezzar that the one true Almighty God is able to protect men from many dangers, God recognizes men of strong faith, and God is loving and faithful to His believers.

Application

God protected Daniel and it is believed that Daniel lived well into his eighties under a number of different rulers. He was a prophet and was known for his wisdom and righteousness.

God will send His angels into difficult situations to protect his believers. When all possible solutions within human reason have been exhausted, God will send His angels to resolve the problem. The issues and problems are never the same and solutions are unique.

It was Daniel's humble and continual prayers that made God respond to Daniel's requests for understanding. God hears our fervent prayers and may respond by sending an angel to communicate information by allowing access to the spiritual realm. Daniel was a faithful servant that spent much of his prayer life on his knees pleading for forgiveness and wisdom.

Jeremiah 29:13 reads, "And ye shall seek me, and find me, when ye shall search for me with all your heart."

Daniel's prayers were heard and God sent his angels to minister so that he may get a better understanding of the spiritual realm.

Daniel 10:10–15 reads, "And, behold, a hand touched me, which set me upon my knees and upon the palms of my hands. And he said unto me, O Daniel, a man greatly beloved, understand the words that I speak unto thee, and stand upright: for unto thee am I now sent. And when he had spoken this word unto me, I stood trembling. Then said he unto me, Fear not, Daniel: for from the first day that thou didst set thine heart to understand, and to chasten thyself before thy God, thy words were heard, and I am come for thy words."

A mighty angel touched Daniel and explained that his words were heard and that this angel was sent to give Daniel the understanding he was seeking. The angel explained that he was delayed due to the fact that he encountered a demon (prince of the kingdom of Persia) and that Michael (one of God's chief angels) was sent to resolve the issue.

The spiritual realm that surrounds us is filled with angels of many different talents, ranks and missions. The fact that angels encounter demons and are at times delayed makes our prayer life even more critical.

Elisha prayed that the Lord would open the eyes of a young servant.

2 Kings 6:17 reads, "And Elisha prayed, and said, Lord I pray thee, open his eyes, that he may see, And the Lord opened the eyes of the young man; and he saw: and, behold, that mountain was full of houses and chariots of fire round about Elisha."

God allowed this young servant Elisha to see the spiritual realm. It was a world that was amazing that was filled with angels and many other things impossible to describe.

The spirit of God teaches us many things that are freely given and are not of this world. The nature man can only see the things of this world as they relate to science and considers all spiritual things as foolish.

1 Corinthians 2:9–10 reads, "But as it is written, Eye hath not seen, not ear heard, neither have entered into the heart of man, the things which God hat prepared for them that loved him. But God hath revealed them unto us by his spirit: for the Spirit searcheth all things, yes, the deep things of God."

Elijah

Approximately (900 BC to 849 BC)

THE NAME ELIJAH MEANS "My God is Yahweh." It is estimated he was born in 900 BC at Tishba in the Gilead region (located in the northern kingdom of Israel) during the time of King Ahab and King Ahaziah. It was said, he was born with an angel at his side that provided a fabric of fire that surrounded him. We are told his appearance was rough due to the fact he lived off the land and would rest in caves. However, he had a relationship with God that few men have ever experienced. As a Jewish priest, Elijah lived a life in complete obedience to God's will that resulted in him seeing and prophesying events that were impossible to be foreseen by any other human being. He grew to be one of the most important prophets in the world and experienced first-hand blessings directly from God.

God used Elijah as a prophet to reveal and communicate His purpose in reflecting His divine glory.

Deuteronomy 18:18-19 reads, "I will raise them up a Prophet from among their brethren, like unto thee, and will put my words in his mouth; and he shall speak unto them all that I shall command him. And it shall come to pass, that whosoever will not hearken unto my words which he shall speak in my name, I will require it of him."

God raised up many prophets among the people for the purpose of providing an intercessor between God and man. Like Moses, God spoke directly to Elijah and directed him as to what to say to King Ahab.

The prophets are classified by the length and scope of the book. The Major Prophets were Isaiah, Jeremiah, and Ezekiel. The twelve Minor Prophets are Hosea, Joel, Amos, Obadiah, Jonah, Micah, Nahum, Habakkuk, Zephaniah, Haggai, Zechariah, and Malachi. Elijah was neither a major nor minor prophet due to the lack of written records. However, Elijah held a prominent position as a prophet due to his unparalleled relationship with God and God's divine plan for mankind.

As Moses, Elijah travels through the wilderness with God's direction and His angels. For 40 days and 40 nights he traveled to Mount Horeb in the Sinai. It is believed this is the same place where God made his covenant with Israel and gave Moses the 10 commandments.

1 Kings 19: 9-10 reads, "And he came thither unto a cave, and lodged there; behold, the word of the Lord came to him, and he said unto him, "What doest thou here, Elijah?" And he said, I have been very jealous for the Lord God of hosts: for the children of Israel have forsaken thy covenant, thrown down thine altars, and slain thy prophets with the sword; and I, even I only, am left; and they seek my life, to take it away."

God asked Elijah what he was doing in this cave as if to say there is much to be done and this was not the way to get His work accomplished. God was very patient and loving with His servant and knew what he had experienced. The Lord is merciful, gracious, longsuffering, and is full of goodness and truth.

1Kings 19:15-16 reads, "And the Lord said unto him, Go, return on thy way to the wilderness of Damascus: and when thou comest, anoint Hazael to be King over Syria. And Jehu the son of Nimshi shalt thou anoint to be king over Israel: and Elisha the son of Shaphat of Abel-meholah shalt thou anoint to be prophet in thy room."

God explained to Elijah he had a great deal of traveling and work to complete. He had to return back to the wilderness and travel hundreds of miles to Damascus to anoint a new King over Syria and to anoint a new King over Israel. On his travels he would also meet Elisha who would eventually replace Elijah as the new prophet to Israel.

At this point, Israel and the Jewish people had a number of enemies in the area that would like to invade Israel and steal her treasures and land. Benhadad the king of Syria (885BC -860BC) had a great army and the support of thirty two other kings in the area. King Benhadad was jealous of Israel's riches and wanted Samaria and its rich land and sent a messenger to King Ahab demanding that King Ahad turn over all his gold and property. King Benhadad and the people of Syria worshiped a number of pagan gods and were greatly dependent on hundreds of false prophets for direction in many areas of their lives. However, God sent an unnamed prophet of God to King Ahab of Israel to explain that God would not allow his army to be defeated by the Syrians. The fact that this prophet told Ahad what was going to happen, makes it impossible for Ahab not to acknowledge it was God who was in control of the outcome of this war. God saved King Ahad from a certain defeat and death. God wanted Ahab and all men to acknowledge that God was in control and to place their trust in Him and not on themselves.

Ahab is also involved in a conflict over a vineyard owned by Naboth. The vineyard was located in Jezreel next to Ahab's palace in Samaria. Ahad wanted to purchase the vineyard, but Naboth refused because it was promised as part of a family inheritance. Ahad was displeased and complained to Jezebel. Jezebel (Satan incarnate) developed a scheme that would place Naboth in a very difficult position. Jezebel paid for witnesses that claimed that Naboth had blasphemed God and the king. The people when they heard of this blasphemy claim took Naboth out of the city and stoned him to death. Due to custom Naboth sons were also killed thereby allowing the King to lay claim to the vineyard.

As with Moses, God required Elijah to confront the ruler of the land, in this case Ahad King of Israel. Elijah found Ahab in the vineyard of Naboth who was killed due to Jezebel's scheming and lying.

1 Kings 21:17-20 reads, "And the word of the Lord came to Elijah the Tishbite, saying, Arise, go down to meet Ahad king of Israel, which is in Samaria: behold, he is in the vineyard of Naboth, whither he is gone down to possess it. And thou shalt speak unto him, saying, Thus saith the Lord, Hast thou killed, and also taken possession? And thou shalt speak unto him, saying, Thus saith the Lord, In the place where dogs licked the blood of Naboth shall dogs lick thy blood, even thine. And Ahab said to Elijah, Hast thou found me, O mine enemy? And he answered, I have found thee: because thou hast sold thyself to work evil in the sight of the Lord."

1 Kings 21: 28-29 reads, "And the word of the Lord came to Elijah the Tishbite, saying. Seest thou how Ahab humbleth himself before me? because he humbleth himself before me, I will not bring the evil in his days: but in his son's days will I bring the evil upon his house."

God was instructing Elijah by saying He will determine how, when, and where Ahab will be confronted by his sins. God is in control and he will determine when evil is released and the penalty for sin is paid. In this case, because Ahab had repented and publically displayed his remorse God did provide a temporary stay. However, Ahab was later killed and his sins were transferred to his sons who were also killed. Confession of our sins and praying for our forgiveness is important aspect of being a Christian.

Elijah

Christians today are under God's grace due to His overwhelming love, love we are not worthy of, and a love we cannot comprehend. God allowed His only Son to die on a cross to give all of mankind the opportunity to spend eternity with Him in heaven. Today we are dependent on the Holy Spirit to help us to recognize our sins and make changes that will place us in communion with our Creator.

After the death of King Ahab, Ahaziah his son assumed control of northern Israel and Jehoshaphat maintains control over Judah. The death of a King would normally leave some vacuum in control and rebellion would normally break out. Mesha king of Moab (area east of the Dead Sea and now western Jordan) was successful in a rebellion over high taxes. Ahaziah became sick and requested an oracle of Baal that was a rebellion to the worship of the God of Israel. It was this rebellion by King Ahaziah and the following of his mother (Jezebel) in the worship of Baal that provoked the anger of the Lord God of Israel.

2 Kings 1:3–4 reads, "But the angel of the Lord said to Elijah the Tishbite, Arise, go up to meet the messengers of the King of Samaria, and say unto them, Is it not because there is not a God in Israel, that ye go to inquire of Baal-zebub the god of Ekron? Now therefore thus saith the Lord, Thou shalt not come down from that bed on which thou art gone up, but shalt surely die. And Elijah departed."

The angel of the Lord speaks directly to Elijah as he did with Moses and commands him to confront King Ahaziah. The angel of the Lord speaks as God, executes the power of God, and identifies himself as God. Those that see him fear for their lives because they recognize the power and presences of God himself. King Ahaziah had deliberately turned from the Lord God of Israel and worshiped Baal for the healing of his aliment. His worship of Baal was responsible for hardening the hearts of the people against the God of Israel.

King Ahaziah sent fifty soldiers after Elijah to punish him for confronting the King of Israel about his idol worship and demand that he repent as did his father Ahab.

2 Kings 1:12 reads, "And Elijah answered and said unto them, If I be a man of God, let fire come down from heaven, and consume thee and thy fifty. And the fire of God came down from heaven, and consumed him and his fifty."

God did work directly through Elijah to deliver His words and response to King Ahaziah's decision to worship pagan idols. God's message was clear when fire poured down to destroy two units of 50 soldiers and His decision to let King Ahaziah die in his bed from his own aliments.

The death of King Ahaziah resulted in Jehoram becoming King of Israel. It is believed that King Jehoram (852BC to 841BC) was the brother of Ahab and was King of the northern kingdom after the death of King Ahaziah.

God at this time reveals to Elijah that he will soon depart from this earth and needs to prepare Elisha to take his place. Elisha's main task would be to carry on Elijah's mission to stop the worship of idols. Elisha then asked Elijah to provide him with a double portion of his spiritual power and understanding. Obviously, this is only possible through God's will.

Elijah's reputation was great among the prophets and he shared his vision with the guild of prophets and priests of Israel. This guild of 50 prophets began to follow Elijah at a distance to both provide protection and to bear witness to the prophecy of his departure.

We are limited in our ability to understand all of God's plans and actions that take place within a man's life here on earth and in heaven. This was especially true of Elijah who like Moses spoke directly with God. Elijah was an extraordinary man that had an extraordinary relationship with God Almighty. He was chosen of God to be His representative and experienced God's protection and care.

2 Kings 2:11 reads, "And it came to pass, as they still went on, and talked, that, behold, there appeared a chariot of fire, and horses of fire, and parted them both asunder; and Elijah went up by a whirlwind into heaven."

God is in control and He will decide what will transpire on earth and within each man's life. In this case, God decided that it was time for Elijah to depart this earth and go to heaven, so He took him. At this time, God determined the mission of confronting the pagan idol worshipers would be passed on to Elisha. So the mission and the mantle were then passed on to Elisha.

Elijah was a man with many human frailties, but his heart and soul was devoted completely to the worship and praise of the Lord God Almighty of Israel. The governments, its rulers, were all corrupt and wanted to continue to enslave it's people to worship Baal and other idols for the purpose of extorting money and other valuables for the promise of good fortune. God knew the heart of Elijah and accepted him as His messenger to deliver God's voice to a people that were lost in the worship of pagan idols.

Application

God loved Elijah regardless of his many human frailties. He was at times completely dependent on God for food, shelter, and protection. His single purpose in life was to please God with His prophecies. He was God's messenger and he was God's humble obedient servant. He was truly a unique individual that lived off the land and took shelter wherever God provided it.

Society and the culture of that day had fallen to great depths. It was common for people to worship idols in the hope of receiving a good crop and healthy animals. Their superstitions made them easy prey for corrupt rulers like King Ahab and Jezebel who promoted this worship of pagan gods by building monuments and temples for Baal and others. In addition, hundreds of priests and oracles were employed to convince people to sacrifice animals, money, and children to these false gods for rain, sun, and prosperity.

Jeremiah

Approximately (650BC to 570BC)

It is believed that Jeremiah was born and grew up in a family that was involved in the Temple at Jerusalem. He was approached by God to become a prophet at an early age. He was outspoken as a child and highly critical of the priests and those involved in the Temple. He was born in the city of Anathoth which was located just north of Jerusalem. His prophetic ministry lasted about 40 years.

Jeremiah 1:5–9 reads, "Before I formed thee in the belly I knew thee; and before thou comest forth out of the womb I sanctified thee, and I ordained thee a prophet unto the nations. Then said I, Ah, Lord God! Behold, I cannot speak: for I am a child. But the Lord said unto me, Say not, I am a child: for thou shalt go to all that I shall send thee, and whatsoever I command thee thou shalt speak. Be not afraid of their faces: for I am with thee to deliver thee, saith the Lord. Then the Lord put forth his hand, and touched my mouth. And the Lord said unto me, Behold, I have put my words in thy mouth."

God's plan for Jeremiah's life as a prophet was determined before Jeremiah's birth. God spoke directly to Jeremiah and explained to him that He (God) would be with him and protect him from his enemies. As Moses and many others, Jeremiah was fearful and did not believe he was capable of handling that much responsibility. Jeremiah was commanded by God to deliver a message that was highly critical of the priests and the people living at that time. The sins of the people would eventually lead to the destruction of Judah.

Jeremiah 32:15 reads, "For thus saith the Lord of hosts, the God of Israel; Houses and fields and vineyards shall be possessed again in this land."

Lamentations 3:21-26 reads, "This I recall to my mind, therefore have I hope. It is of the Lord's mercies that we are not consumed, because his compassions fail not. They are new every morning: great is thy faithfulness. The Lord is my portion, saith my soul; therefore will I hope in him. The Lord is good unto them that wait for him, to the soul that seeketh him. It is good that a man should both hope and quietly wait for the salvation of the Lord."

Jeremiah was a strong and courageous prophet who trusted in God for his wisdom and direction. Even under great social pressure for his strong criticism of the worship of false gods, Jeremiah remained hopeful of God's love and mercies. He knew that God had a plan for his life and that life would not end in emptiness but would continue in rejoicing for eternity.

Jeremiah's hope for the future was based on the new covenant found in the New Testament.

Jeremiah 31:31-33 reads, "Behold, the days come, saith the Lord, that I will make a new covenant with the house of Israel, and with the house of Judah: Not according to the covenant that I made with their fathers in the day that I took them by the hand to bring them out of the land of Egypt; which my covenant they brake, although I was a husband unto them, saith the Lord: But this shall be the covenant that I will make with the house of Israel; After those days, saith the Lord, I will put my law in their inward parts, and write it in their hearts: and will be their God, and they shall be my people."

The new covenant is God's invitation to all of mankind that God is waiting to give to all of mankind eternal life with the indwelling of the Holy Spirit. God's New Covenant will forgive all of man's sins and remember them no more. The penalty for all of man's sin will be paid with the death and resurrection of God's Son, Jesus Christ. All these blessings are available to anyone who believes in God and His saving grace.

Application

As a prophet, Jeremiah was God's messenger. The messages that he delivered were highly critical of the temple priests and the evil practices that took place in Jerusalem, Judea, and Israel. The worship of idols and other false gods were common practices along with the inability to recognize sin and lack of repentance.

Today, we still have the worship of false gods and the lack of repentance. Jeremiah's life as a messenger was difficult due to the refusal of the people to follow God's commands. God spoke directly to Jeremiah and blessed him. God spoke through Jeremiah to deliver a message of condemnation and hope. These messages were met with anger, hate, and physical harm.

Even though Jeremiah was hated and mistreated, God continued to speak through Jeremiah and protect him. Like Jeremiah, the messages we deliver may not be accepted and may be met with hate and ridicule. However, our Master is the one true God who is the Creator of all and His plan for our life is waiting for us to fulfill. Our understanding of God and His plan for mankind is limited and requires us to place our trust in Him each day.

We live in a fallen world that is filled with disease, natural disasters, sin, and evil. As Jeremiah, we place our trust in God and His promises.

Jeremiah 29:11–12 reads, "For I know the thoughts that I think toward you, saith the Lord, thoughts of peace, and not of evil, to give you an expected end. Then shall ye call upon me, and ye shall go and pray unto me, and I will hearken unto you."

The Christian loves God and is happy to commune with Him each day in prayer. God is in the thoughts of a Christian's daily life and his life is a sacrifice to his Lord and Savior. His purpose as a Christian is to share God's grace and love to those around him and to lessen the sorrows and pain of a fallen world.

Joseph (the Father of Jesus)

Approximately (30 BC to 25 AD)

THE ANGEL OF THE Lord appeared to Joseph four times in a dream. In the first dream, the angel explained that Joseph should take Mary as his wife due to the fact she was conceived by the Holy Spirit. In the second dream, the angel told Joseph to take Mary and Jesus and flee to Egypt. In the third dream, the angel told Joseph to travel to Israel due to the fact those that sought to kill Jesus are no longer living. In the fourth dream, God warns Joseph not to go to Judea, but to remain in Galilee and Nazareth.

Joseph was a righteous man who followed the instructions given to him in the dreams without question.

Application

We are to live a righteous life like Joseph and follow God's instruction without question. In this situation, an angel appeared to Joseph in a number of dreams that detailed instructions as to how, where and when to travel to avoid danger. An angel may appear in our dreams that may instruct us as to how to avoid danger. In other words, an angel may communicate with us through a dream that may result in providing protection. Making the right decision can be extremely difficult due to the fact we are normally not aware of all the facts, we are only aware of past and the present, and have no idea of any future events.

Angels are mentioned in the Bible over 270 times. They have been responsible for delivering many important messages, providing protection, destroying armies, destroying evil angels, and carrying out many other of God's commands and wishes. Some of these angels may be with us from the day of our birth until the last day of our life. During the period of time we spend on the earth we may be in the company of hundreds or thousands of angels. There are times when they place their arms on our shoulder and comfort us in times of great distress. Their presence may bring peace to a troubled heart and comfort to a mind under stress.

John the Baptist

Approximately (1 BC to 36 AD)

JOHN THE BAPTIST WAS one of God's messengers. His message was that the Messiah was coming and that it was time to repent of your sins and to be obedient to God's law. Jesus did meet John the Baptist and asked John to baptize Him to fulfill God's will for his life.

John the Baptist's father was Zechariah a priest and husband to Elizabeth. Elizabeth was a relative of Mary the mother of Jesus.

Luke 1:13 reads, "But the angel said unto him, Fear not, Zechariah: for thy prayer is heard; and thy wife Elisabeth shall bear thee a son, and thou shalt call his name John."

Like 1:19 reads, "And the angel answering said unto him, I am Gabriel, that stand in the presence of God; and am sent to speak unto thee, and to show thee these glad tidings."

God was preparing and planning for the baptism of Jesus Christ and the beginning of His ministry.

Matthew 3:13–15 reads, "Then cometh Jesus from Galilee to Jordan unto John, to be baptized of him. But John forbade him, saying, I have need to be baptized of thee, and comest thou to me? And Jesus answering said unto him, Suffer it to be so now: for thus it becometh us to fulfill all righteousness. Then he suffered him."

John the Baptist knew who Jesus was and felt unworthy to baptize Jesus. However, Jesus needed to be obedient to God's will for His life and to be identified with all of man's sin. Jesus would carry all of man's sin to the cross.

Matthew 3:16–17 reads, "And Jesus, when he was baptized, went up straightway out of the water: and, lo, the heavens were opened unto him, and he saw the spirit of God descending like a dove, and lighting upon him:

And lo a voice from heaven, saying, This is my beloved Son, in whom I am well pleased."

This baptism of Jesus was an important part of Jesus' ministry and was recognized with God's verbal approval directly from heaven.

Jesus appeared to the eleven disciples after his death and spoke of the great commission.

Matthew 28:19–20 reads, "Go ye therefore, and teach all nations, baptizing them in the name of the Father, and of the Son, and of the Holy Ghost; Teaching them to observe all things whatsoever I have commanded you: and , lo, I am with you always, even unto the end of the world, Amen."

God's command to be baptized was initiated with John the Baptist. Jesus followed God's will and was baptized and commanded his disciples to go out and teach all nations, baptizing them in the name of the Father, the Son, and Holy Spirit.

Application

John the Baptist was a messenger from God. The angel Gabriel appeared before John's father and said that his prayers for a son would be answered and he should be called, John. John the Baptist's mission would be to travel, teach, baptize and prepare the way for Jesus.

Jesus' life is an example for all of mankind. Jesus began his ministry by being baptized in the Jordan River by John the Baptist. It is believed Jesus traveled about thirty miles from Nazareth to Al-Maghtas, Jordan to be baptized by John the Baptist. Being baptized is an important part of being recognized as a Christian. Jesus was baptized as an example to all of mankind.

According to Jewish law and tradition a Priest needed to be 30 years of age before he could be anointed. It is believed that Jesus was about 30 years of age when he was baptized.

The act of making a decision to become a Christian requires that a person follow God's word and commands. The process begins with admitting that you are a sinner and that you are in need of forgiveness for those sins. This is a lifelong process that requires a great deal of dedication to following God's word.

Jesus lived His life as an example for all of mankind. Baptism is a ceremony that all Christians can experience. During Jesus baptism the heavens open up and the Spirit of God descended upon Jesus. As the water rushes over your body your soul is renewed. It is at this moment of great joy that your soul is filled with a new life and craves to be united with its' Creator. John the Baptist had firsthand experience as he watched the Holy Spirit descend from heaven and rest upon Jesus the Lamb of God.

John 1:32 reads, "And John bare record, saying, I saw the Spirit descending from heaven like a dove, and it abode upon him."

The Spirit of God descends from heaven and seals the soul of each person forever who is baptized in the name of the Father, Son, and Holy Spirit.

Mark 16:14–15 reads, "Afterward he appeared unto the eleven as they sat at meat, and upbraided them with their unbelief and hardness of heart, because they believed not them which had seen him after he was risen. And he said unto them, Go ye into all the world, and preach the gospel to every creature. He that believeth and is baptized shall be saved; but he that believeth not shall be damned."

The result of not believing is Jesus Christ, His death, and resurrection is death. Man needs to repent of his sins and completely embrace God's love and forgiveness. A person who makes a decision to follow Jesus will be identified by baptism and receive the Holy Spirit.

Romans 6:3–4 reads, "Know ye not, that so many of us as were baptized into Jesus Christ were baptized into his death? Therefore we are buried with him by baptism into death: that like as Christ was raised up from the dead by the glory of the Father, even so we also should walk in newness of life."

John the Baptist's message is that man needs to repent of his sins, believe in the Messiah, and be baptized.

Peter the Apostle

Approximately (1 BC to 64 AD)

PETER (SIMON) THE APOSTLE (1 BC to 64 AD) had one brother Andrew who also became an Apostle and a follower of Jesus the Christ. It is believed Peter wrote the Gospel of Mark with the assistance of John Mark. It is also generally believed he wrote the First and Second Epistle of Peter. He was a fisherman with little formal education, lived in the village of Bethsaida, and worked in Capernaum with fishing nets on the Sea of Galilee. He was married, worked with his father (Jona) and brother, Andrew in a physically demanding job with long hours. Generally, Simon (Peter) was considered to be an out spoken man who felt free to share his opinions and at times a little rough around the edges. The area was considered to be in extreme poverty with a strong sense of independence from Jerusalem.

The first mention of Simon (Peter) is after Jesus is baptized on the Jordan River south of the Sea of Galilee. It appears both Peter and Andrew were both associated with John the Baptist and his ministry. When John the Baptist met Jesus he knew who Jesus was and immediately called Him the Lamb of God. It is also possible that John the Baptist may have been aware of Jesus of Nazareth from relatives and other acquaintances. It should be noted Peter, Andrew and Jesus were about around thirty years of age with Andrew being the youngest.

John 1:35-42 reads, "Again the next day after John stood, and two of his disciples; And looking upon Jesus as he walked, he saith, Behold the Lamb of God! And two disciples heard him speak, and they followed Jesus. And Jesus turned, and saw them following, and saith unto them, "What seek ye?" They said unto him, Rabbi, (which is to say, being interpreted, Master), where dwellest thou? He saith unto them, "Come and see." They came and saw where he dwelt, and abode with him that day: for it was about the tenth hour. One of the two which heard John speak, and followed him, was Andrew, Simon Peter's brother. He first findeth his own brother Simon, and saith unto him, We have found the Messiah, which is, being interpreted, the Christ. And he brought him to Jesus. And when Jesus beheld him, he said, Thou art Simon the son of Jona, thou shalt be called Cephas, which is by interpretation, A stone."

This first meeting between Peter, Andrew and Jesus resulted in Andrew and Peter deciding to become more involved with the ministry of Jesus of Nazareth. Jesus knew Simon (Peter) and knew that Peter would be a leader for the Apostles and the foundation of Christ's church.

The next time we learn of Simon (Peter) he is in Capernaum or Bethsaida fishing with his partners the sons of Zebedee, John and James.

Luke 5: 1–10 reads, "And it came to pass, that, as the people pressed upon him to hear the word of God, he stood by the lake of Gennesaret. And saw two ships standing by the lake: but the fishermen were gone out of them, and were washing their nets. And he entered into one of the ships, which were Simon's, and prayed him that he would thrust out a little from the land. And he sat down, and taught the people out of the ship. Now when he had left speaking, he said unto Simon, "Launch out into the deep, and let down your nets for a draught." And Simon answering said unto him, Master, we have toiled all night, and have taken nothing: nevertheless at thy word I will let down the net. And when they had this done, they enclosed a great multitude of fishes: and their net brake. And they beckoned unto their partners, which were in the other ship, that they should come and help them. And they came, and filled both ships, so that they began to sink. When Simon Peter saw it, he fell down at Jesus' knees, saying, Depart from me; for I am a sinful man, O Lord. For he was astonished, and all that were with him, at the draught of the fishes which they had taken: And so was also James, and John, the sons of Zebedee, which were partners with Simon. And Jesus said unto Simon, "Fear not; from henceforth thou shalt catch men."

At this time Jesus steps into Peter's boat due to the crowds of people and asks Peter to take them out a few feet so that He may continue to preach to the people on the shore. Jesus continues His preaching of the gospel as Simon Peter listens. After which, Jesus tells Peter to move his boat out to deeper water and cast his nets. Peter explains he had fished all night and there were no fish to be caught. However, Peter obeys Jesus' wishes and goes out to deeper water and lets down his nets. And, to his surprise he nets so many fish that he asks John and James to bring out their boat to help pull in all the fish. Both boats worked together landing the fish to the point to where both boats began to sink. The reality of the situation hits Peter hard to the point to where he realizes he is in the presence of a miracle and God's messenger. Peter falls at the feet of Jesus and asks that Jesus leave him due to the sin in his life. He feels he is not worthy to be in the presence of Jesus and asks that Jesus depart from him. Satan (fallen man, natural man) is at work with Peter trying to convince him not to follow Jesus because of his sin. Peter physically was a strong man capable of pulling in large heavy nets filled with fish, but spiritually he was weak and was overcome by fear of failure. Jesus knew that Peter would grow to be a great disciple and continued to love him and work with him regardless of his human frailties. God shows that same love and patience today as we wrestle with fear and strive to grow in faith.

Next we find Jesus at Peter's mother-in-law's house. She is sick and needs immediate attention.

Luke 4:38–39 reads, "And he arose out of the synagogue, and entered into Simon's house. And, Simon's wife's mother was taken with a great fever; and they besought him for her. And he stood over her, and rebuked the fever; and it left her: and immediately she arose and ministered unto them."

Peter is present with Jesus as He rebukes the fever and allows Peter's wife's mother to continue with her life. As they continue their travels Peter's knowledge and understanding of Jesus' ministry grows stronger to the point Peter becomes the lead apostle.

Mark 3:13–19 reads, "And he goeth up into a mountain, and calleth unto him whom he would and they came unto him. And he ordained twelve, that they should be with him, and that he might send them forth to preach. And to have power to heal sicknesses, and to cast out devils; And Simon the surnamed Peter; And James the son of Zebedee, and John the brother of James; and he surnamed them Boanerges, which is, the sons of thunder. And Andrew, and Philip, and Bartholomew, and Matthew, and Thomas, and James the son of Alphaeus, and Thaddeus, and Simon the Canaanite, And Judas Iscariot, which also betrayed him: and they went into a house."

Jesus goes to the mountain to pray and make the decision as to who would be ordained to be His disciples. Simon Peter is the first to be considered and the first to be ordained to be one of Jesus' disciples. Obviously, Peter is held in high regard as a leader and that Jesus would delegate great responsibility and power to heal the sick and cast out demons. Peter was a follower who was eager to learn and who was quick to assume more responsibility over the next two years.

God had a covenant with the Jewish people and wanted to ensure that they were the first to hear the good news that Jesus was the Messiah. Peter and the disciples first mission was to go out into the Jewish community by twos to preach that Jesus was the Messiah, heal the sick, and cast out demons. Peter leads the disciples as they travel from village to village preaching that Jesus is the Messiah.

Mark 5:37–43 reads, "And he suffered no man to follow him, save Peter, and James, and John the brother of James. And he cometh to the house of the ruler of the synagogue, and seeth the tumult, and them that wept and wailed greatly. And when he was come in, he said unto them, "Why make ye this ado, and weep? The damsel is not dead, but sleepeth." And they laughed him to scron. But when he had put them all out, he taketh the father and the mother of the damsel, and them that were with him, and entereth in where the damsel was lying. And he took the damsel by the hand, and said unto her, "Talitha cumi"; which is, being interpreted, "Damsel," (I say unto thee,) "arise." And straightway the damsel arose, and walked; for she was of the age of twelve years. And they were astonished with a great astonishment. And he charged them straitly that no man should know it; and commanded that something should be given her to eat."

Jesus required that Peter, James, and John be present at this miracle for their own enrichment and for a number of other reasons. These Apostles had to experience and realize the full impact that Jesus was God and that God has power over sin, disease, death, and Satan. They were to act as witnesses to Jesus' Transfiguration and later to Jesus' Ascension. There is no limitation to God's power and the Apostles needed to realize that this power was available through faith. The miracles that Jesus completed were in the presence of faith, for building faith, and for proclaiming that Jesus was the Messiah.

A transformation took place within Peter that changed him from an outspoken rough man of thunder, to a humble obedient servant of the Lord God Almighty even to death. He rejoiced the day of his death that he would now be reunited with his Savior that had been crucified over 30 years prior.

Matthew 16:13–16 reads, "When Jesus came into the coasts of Caesarea Philippi, he asked his disciples, saying, "Whom do men say that I the Son of man am?" And they said, Some say that thou art John the Baptist: some, Elijah; and others, Jeremiah, or one of the prophets. He saith unto them, "But whom say ye that I am?" And Simon Peter answered and said, Thou art the Christ, the Son of the living God. And Jesus answered and said unto him, "Blessed art thou, Simon Bar-jona: for flesh and blood hath not revealed it unto thee, but my Father which is in heaven. And I say also unto thee, That thou art Peter, and upon this rock I will build my church; and the gates of hell shall not prevail against it. And I will give unto thee the keys of the kingdom of heaven: and whatsoever thou shalt bind on earth shall be bond in heaven: and whatsoever thou shalt loose on earth shall be loosed in heaven."

Caesarea Philippi is a city located about 120 miles northeast of Jerusalem at the foot of Mount Hermon. The location provides a contrast between Jesus the Messiah and the local culture that is buried in the superstition and acts of pure evil related to the worship of many gods. Herod the Great built a temple near the Mount to celebrate Caesar Augustus, hence the name Caesarea Philippi. Jesus takes the Apostles on the twenty five mile journey from Galilee to Caesarea Philippi for the purpose of allowing them to be free of the daily distractions and to concentrate on their mission with Jesus. When Jesus asked the question, "But whom say ye that I am?" It is only Peter that responses without hesitation and said, Thou art the Christ, the Son of the living God. It was Peter that reached that level of spiritual discernment and allowed him to freely identify Jesus' deity as being God's Son.

God blessed Peter throughout his life for his faith, for his discernment, and for his unwavering faithfulness. It was Peter and his testimony that God used as the rock that lead the disciples and provided a foundation for the church. Jesus is the Messiah and through Him God is keeping His promise to provide a Savior for all of mankind. God at this point is giving Peter more responsibility and authority for building the church.

God promised to give Peter the keys to heaven that will allow him to enter heaven. This was only possible because of his confession of faith and the confession of faith by all the Apostles. The confession of faith also resulted in God also giving Peter and the Apostles the authority to bind and loose the church with respect to daily issues that needed to be addressed. Jesus left Peter and the Apostles on earth with God's authority to continue to build the church and to preach that God gave the ultimate sacrifice for our sins and that was the life of His only Son, Jesus. Confession of faith by man is the only possible way to spend eternity with your Creator.

Roman rule over Israel was severe and the penalty for a convicted criminal was death on a cross. The convicted criminal was required to carry their cross to the place of crucifixion. This was a long and painful death that may last three or four days. To the common man at that time the cross meant only one thing, a long and painful death. Peter may have thought Jesus was there to rescue them from this oppressive Roman rule and become king of Israel.

Consequently, when Peter heard Jesus explain he was going to die and rise on the third day he was bewildered. Peter was a bold and impetuous Apostle who did not hesitate to challenge Jesus when he spoke of His own death.

Matthew 16: 22-23 reads, "Then Peter took Him, and began to rebuke him, saying, Be it far from thee, Lord: this shall and be unto thee. But he turned, and said unto Peter, "Get thee behind me, Satan: thou art an offense unto me: for thou savorest not the things that be of God, thou those that be of men."

Peter's reaction reveals that he did not fully understand the purpose for Jesus' death and resurrection. Peter is going through a transformation from a natural man with many frailties to a spiritual man. Jesus sees that Satan is once again trying to tempt Him from carrying out God's promise to provide salvation for all of mankind. Jesus was also teaching that there is a cost related to discipleship and that cost may involve losing your life.

Matthew 16:24 reads, Then said Jesus unto his disciples, "If any man will come after me, let him deny himself, and take up his cross, and follow me."

Jesus was telling his Apostles that they need to realize that there is a cost related to following Him. Peter and the Apostles were learning that following Jesus would involve a cost and part of that cost would be to deny self.

Jesus, Peter, and the Apostles traveled to Jerusalem where the final days unfolded for Jesus' life.

Matthew 26:40 reads, "And he cometh unto the disciples, and findeth them asleep, and saith unto Peter, What, could ye not watch with me one hour?"

Gethsemane was a beautiful garden on the slopes of the Mount of Olives that was used as a place for rest and reflection. It was a perfect place for Jesus, Peter, and the disciples to pray. Peter and the disciples again showed their human weakness when Jesus finds them sleeping rather than praying. Even during this final hour of greatest need, Peter fails to keep watch and pray.

During this late hour of darkness Judas, Malchus (servant of the high priest), and a number of the soldiers slithered into the gardens to betray and arrest Jesus.

John 18:10 reads, "Then Simon Peter having a sword drew it, and smote the high priest's servant, and cut off his right ear. The servant's name was Malchus."

Peter again was quick to react and was willing to defend Jesus with his sword. He was highly capable physically and knew how to defend himself and Jesus with a sword. Peter was capable of being very loyal to Jesus, but at times was rash and hasty. It seems his formal training was limited and he did make mistakes at times, but he did assume responsibility readily and did have natural leadership skills.

One of Peter's greatest failures was when he denies Jesus three times.

Mark 14: 66–72 reads, "And as Peter was beneath in the palace, there cometh one of the maids of the high priest. And when she saw Peter warming himself, she looked upon him, and said, And thou also was with Jesus of Nazareth. But he denied, saying, I know not, neither understand I what thou sayest. And he went out into the porch; and the cock crew. And a maid saw him again, and began to say to them that stood by, This is one of them. And he denied it again, And a little after, they that stood by said again to Peter, Surely thou art one of them: for thou art a Galilean, and thy speech thereto. But he began to curse and to swear, saying, I know not this man of whom ye speak. And the second time the cock crew. And Peter called to mind the word that Jesus said unto him, Before the cock crew twice, thou shalt deny me thrice. And when he thought thereon, he wept."

Peter was present as the high priest began to question Jesus at the palace. Peter sat with the servants so as not to be detected and to listen and watch the hearing conducted by the Sanhedrin. The witnesses against Jesus were for the most part conflicting and not enough to convict Jesus of any crime. However, the high priest began to ask Jesus if he was the Christ the Son of the Blessed. Until this point Jesus had said nothing.

Mark 14: 62 reads, "And Jesus said, I am: and ye shall see the Son of man sitting on the right hand of power, and coming in the clouds of heaven."

Jesus in this statement provides the information that is needed to convict him of blasphemy and the death penalty. Peter was listening intently and must have been completely demoralized when he heard Jesus speak and the sentence of death that was issued. Peter could no longer protect his

Savior with his might and sword. Fear (Satan) took hold and Peter tried to hide in the crowds, however, he was spotted and questioned a few times if he was a follower of Jesus. His desire to survive overtook him and he lied when he said he did not know Jesus three times before the cock crowed twice. At that moment in time Peter recalled what Jesus had said and he left and wept bitterly.

After the crucifixion, Peter and the other disciples were in great distress and in hiding not sure if they would be next. Mary Magdalene was the first at the grave site in the early morning hours.

John 20:1–7 reads, "The first day of the week cometh Mary Magdalene early, when it was yet dark, unto the sepulcher, and seeth the stone taken away from the sepulcher. Then she runneth, and cometh to Simon Peter, and to the other disciple, whom Jesus loved, and said unto them, They have taken away the Lord out of the sepulcher, and we know not where they have laid him. Peter therefore went forth, and that other disciple, and came to the sepulcher. So they ran both together: and the other disciples did outrun Peter, and came first to the sepulcher. And he stooping down, and looking in, saw the linen clothes lying; yet went he not in. Then cometh Simon Peter following him, and went into the sepulcher, and seeth the linen clothes lie. And the napkin, that was about his head, not lying with the linen clothes, but wrapped together in a place by itself."

After discovering the grave was open Mary Magdalene ran straight for Peter the beloved disciple. Even though Peter had failed miserably he was still held in high regard by all the disciples. Peter was greatly loved by God regardless of his many failures.

Again, we see the eminence of Peter as he is the first to witness the risen Savior among the disciples.

Peter as head of the church and beloved of God was the first to see the risen Lord and Savior. Jesus' second appearance was in a locked room with the eleven disciples.

Luke 24:36–43 reads, "And as they thus spake, Jesus himself stood in the midst of them, and saith unto them, Peace be unto you. But they were terrified and affrighted, and supposed that they had seen a spirit. And he said unto them, Why are ye troubled? and why do thoughts arise in your hearts? Behold my hands and my feet, that it is I myself: handle me, and see; for a spirit hath not flesh and bones, as ye see me have. And when he had thus spoken, he showed them his hands and his feet. And while they yet believed not for joy, and wondered, he said unto them, Have ye here any meat. And they gave him a piece of a broiled fish, and of a honeycomb. And he took it, and did eat before them."

Jesus' second appearance was before his eleven Apostles in a room that had been locked from the inside. In a moment Jesus appeared standing before his disciples in a body that appeared as any other with both skin and bones. In fact, He invited his disciples to examine his hands and feet to verify that it was his body that was crucified on the cross. He also ate fish and honey. This appearance by Jesus in front of his disciples gave them no room for doubt that Jesus had died and then rose from the grave. It was God's grace that allowed for the repentance and remission of sin for all of mankind. Peter and all the disciples were at this time commissioned by God to preach the saving grace of Jesus beginning with Jerusalem and then all the nations.

John 20: 21–23 reads, "Then said Jesus to them again, Peace be unto you: as my Father hath sent me, even so send I you. And when he had said this, he breathed on them, and saith unto them, Receive ye the Holy Ghost: Whosoever sins ye remit, they are remitted unto them, and whosesoever sins ye retain, they are retained."

Peter and the Apostles were given the Holy Spirit to continue the work of Jesus and the preaching of the good news that Jesus had risen and had defeated death for all of mankind. The disciples were now preaching that Jesus was the ultimate sacrifice or all man's sin. The church and its' people may now receive the forgiveness of their sins by believing in the death and resurrection of Jesus, God's only Son.

Peter had failed and denied he knew Jesus three times after Jesus was found guilty of blasphemy and was sentenced to death. Jesus, after His resurrection confronts Peter three times with the same question.

John 21:15–17 reads, "So when they had dined, Jesus saith to Simon Peter, "Simon son of Jonah, lovest thou me more than these? He said unto him, Yea, Lord; you knowest that I love thee. He saith unto him, Feed my lambs. He said to him again the second time, Simon, son of Jonah, lovest thou me? He said unto him, Yea, Lord; thou knowest that I love thee. He saith unto him, Feed my sheep. He saith unto him the third time, Simon, son of Jonah, lovest thou me? Peter was grieved because he said unto him the third time, Lovest thou me? And he said unto him, Lord, thou knowest all things: thou knowest that I love thee. Jesus saith unto him, Feed my sheep."

Peter is confronted by Jesus asking him if he loved his Savior, Jesus. The questions by Jesus and the answers by Peter are heard by all and there is now no doubt that Peter has confirmed and committed to completing his mission to preach the gospel. Peter, the head of the church and commissioned by God still failed and still had lapses in judgment. Peter's journey and all of mans journeys are not without daily challenges due to the old natural man and Satan. However, God does not fail us, His grace and forgiveness is never ending and is available to all those who repent.

Jesus' challenge to Peter is that if he loves Him he needs to feed His sheep. It is not uncommon for sheep to wander while they are grazing and will at times get lost. They have no sense of direction and if they become lost they cannot find their way back to the flock. Man has no sense of spiritual direction and if he becomes lost he needs someone to help him find his way back to his Master and Lord. Sheep are completely defenseless, without sharp teeth, sharp claws, or the speed to escape an attack from a wolf or mountain lion. It is important for sheep to stay close to their shepherd for protection. The same is true for man. Man needs to stay close to God on a daily basis to be able to consume spiritual food and water to maintain enough strength to withstand the attacks from Satan and his demons.

Jesus was not only commanding Peter to feed his sheep and the church, but to maintain a close daily relationship with God that would provide the strength to withstand the relentless attacks from Satan and his demons. Man has a soul that is completely dependent on spiritual nourishment. This nourishment comes from only one source and that one source is God that transforms the soul in daily prayer and study.

Peter at this point was growing in strength and power as the Holy Spirit took on a greater role in his life. Peter's message to the people of Jerusalem had a huge impact and many believed in the message of the cross.

Acts 2:14–36 reads, "But Peter, standing up with the eleven, lifted up his voice, and said unto them, ye men of Judea, and all that dwell at Jerusalem, be this known unto you, and hearken to my words: For these are not drunken, as ye suppose, seeing it is but the third hour of the day. But this is that which was spoken by the prophet Joel; And it shall come to pass in the last days, saith God, I will pour out of my spirit upon all flesh: and your sons and your daughters shall prophesy, and your young men shall see visions, and your old men shall dream dreams: and on my servants and on my handmaidens I will pour out in those days of my spirit; and they shall prophesy: and I will show wonders in heaven above, and signs in the earth beneath: blood, and fire, and vapor of smoke: the sun shall be turned into darkness, and the moon into blood, before that great and notable day of the Lord come: and it shall come to pass, that whosoever shall call on the name of the Lord shall be saved. Ye men of Israel, hear these words; Jesus of Nazareth, a man approved of God among you by miracles and wonders and signs, which God did by him in the midst of you, as ye yourselves also know: Him, being delivered by the determinate counsel and foreknowledge of God, ye have taken, and by wicked hands have crucified and slain: Whom God hath raised up, having loosed the pains of death: because it was not possible that he should be holden of it. For David speaketh concerning him, I foresaw the Lord always before my face; for he is on my right hand, that I should not be moved: Therefore did my heart rejoice, and my tongue was glad, moreover also my flesh shall rest in hope: because thou wilt not leave my soul in hell, neither wilt thou suffer thine holy one to see corruption. Thou hast made known to me the ways of life; thou shalt make me full of joy with thy countenance. Men and brethren, let me freely speak unto you of the patriarch David, that he is both dead and buried, and his sepulcher is with us unto this day. Therefore being a prophet, and knowing that God had sworn with an oath to him, that of the fruit of his loins, according to the flesh, he would raise up Christ to sit on his throne. He seeing this before spake of the resurrection of Christ, that his soul was not left in hell, neither his flesh did see corruption. This Jesus hath God raised up, whereof we all are witnesses. Therefore being by the right hand of God exalted and having received of the Father the promise of the Holy Ghost, he hath shed forth this, which ye now see and hear. For David is not ascended into the heaven: but he saith himself, the Lord saith unto my Lord, sit thou on my right hand, until I make thy foes thy footstool. Therefore let all the house of Israel know assuredly, that God hath made that same Jesus, whom ye have crucified, both Lord and Christ."

The Holy Spirit on the day of Pentacost filled Peter and caused him to deliver a message so strong that it converted over 3,000 people to the belief in Jesus Christ as the risen Savior for all of mankind. Peter spoke of the fulfillment of the prophecy that Jesus would come to be the sacrifice for all of man's sins, that his works and His resurrection would attest that He was the Messiah. He was condemned and crucified by Jewish and Roman Courts for confessing to the truth that He was the Messiah. He was ascended into heaven to sit at God's right hand and has now sent the Holy Spirit to direct and strengthen our spirits. Jesus our glorified Messiah has poured forth the

Holy Spirit. We pray today for the out pouring of the Holy Spirit for the spiritual conversions of millions of people whose spirit is either consumed by self or lost to the desire of money and power.

Peter's spirit and spiritual life was growing in strength to the point of allowing the Holy Spirit to perform miracles through him.

Acts 9:39–43 reads, "Then Peter arose and went with them. When he was come, they brought him into the upper chamber: and all the widows stood by him weeping, and showing the coats and garments which Dorcas made, while she was with them. But Peter put them all forth, and kneeled down, and prayed; and turning him to the body said, Tabitha, arise. And she opened her eyes, and when she saw Peter, she sat up. And he gave her his hand, and lifted her up, and when he has called the saints and widows, presented her alive. And it was known throughout all Joppa; and many believed in the Lord. And it came to pass, that he tarried many days in Joppa with one Simon a tanner."

This first and most powerful miracle performed by an Apostle was completed by Peter. This miracle further confirmed Peter's position as leader of the Apostles. In addition, Peter spent some time in Joppa with Simon the tanner, preaching and teaching to both Jews and Gentiles.

The second miracle related to Peter was the conversion of a Gentile, a Roman centurion. Peter was contacted by Cornelius, a centurion living in Caesarea a city located north of Joppa on the Mediterranean Sea. Cornelius was visited by an angel who told him to contact Peter. So Cornelius summoned Peter to come to Caesarea.

Acts 10:25–28 reads, "And as Peter was coming in, Cornelius met him, and fell down at his feet, and worshiped him. But Peter took him up, saying, Stand up: I myself also am a man. And as he talked with him, he went in, and found many that were come together. And he said unto them, Ye know how that it is an unlawful thing for a man that is a Jew to keep company, or come unto one of another nation; but God hath showed me that I should not call any man common or unclean."

Peter again realized with God's assistance that God was no respecter of people. There is no place in Christianity for prejudice against another man regardless if he is a Gentile or Jew. God accepts all men from all nations who believe in Him, love Him, and obey Him.

Peter's words were revolutionary and moved the church into the worldwide mission of providing the saving Grace in the faith of the Lord Jesus Christ. The Holy Spirit came upon all that heard Peter's message and believed. All men are equal in God's sight. It is man's decision to either accept judgment or salvation. Salvation is faith that is based on the belief on the risen Savior, Jesus Christ, God's only Son.

As Peter's reputation began to grow; so did resentment grow among the Jews and the Romans against the early church.

Acts 12: 1–3 reads, "Now about that time Herod the King stretched forth his hands to vex certain of the church. And he killed James the brother of John with the sword. And because he saw it pleased the Jews, he proceeded further to take Peter also. Then were the days of unleavened bread."

King Herod Agrippa 1 was under pressure due to a famine and decided to blame the church for Israel's problems. King Agrippa 1 was aware of the Jewish resentment of the early Christian church and took advantage of every opportunity to curry favor of the Jews. In this case, the King found that it pleased the Jews when he executed James (son of Zebedee and brother of John) with a sword, so Herod imprisoned Peter. A public trial would allow all the Jews to express their hatred for the early Christian church and increase Herod's status in Jerusalem.

Peter was placed in chains and under heavy guard twenty four hours a day.

Acts 12:7–8 reads, "And behold, the angel of the Lord came upon him, and a light shinned in the prison: and he smote Peter on the side, and raised him up, saying, Arise up quickly, And his chains fell from his hands. And the angel said unto him, Gird thyself, and bind on thy sandals. And so he did. And he saith unto him, Cast thy garment about thee, and follow me."

Even though Peter was under heavy guard and in chains, they were not enough to prevent God from freeing Peter from this prison. It was God's angel that took the chains from Peter, prevented the guards from acting, and opened the gates without keys. Peter was free from certain death and returned to the house of Mary (John Mark's house). The first response from the household was it must be Peter's angel. Peter told the household to tell James (Jesus half brother) what had transpired and that he was free. Peter left the area and began his ministry possibly to Asia Minor.

The Apostle Peter also encountered some conflict when he traveled to Antioch where he was confronted by Paul for not eating with the Gentiles.

Galatians 2:11–13 reads, "But when Peter was come to Antioch, I withstood him to the face, because he was to be blamed. For before that certain came from James, he did eat with the Gentiles: but when they were come, he withdrew and separated himself, fearing them which were of the circumcision. And the other Jews dissembled likewise with him; insomuch that Barnabas also was carried away with their dissimulation."

Again, God is patience with Peter as he tried to understand the relationship between the Jew and Gentile. Peter a Jew, was struggling with following Jewish law and at the same time did not want to offend the Gentiles and Paul a Roman by birth. Paul and the Gentiles are not bound by Jewish law and are equal to all men in God's eye.

Galatians 2:16 reads, "Knowing that a man is not justified by the works of the law, but by the faith of Jesus Christ, even we have believed in Jesus Christ, that we might be justified by the faith of Christ, and not by works of the law: for by the works of the law shall no flesh be justified."

Again, God reminds Peter that his salvation is only possible by the atoning death of his only Son. A believer in Jesus Christ lives a life that glorifies God by obeying, serving, and praising God for his countless blessings. Salvation cannot be achieved by performing good works or by obeying the Jewish law. Salvation is only possible by believing in the death and resurrection of God's only Son, the Lord Jesus Christ.

Application

God loved Peter regardless of his many human frailties and failures. God took Peter a fisherman from Galilee with little formal education and built the Christian church with the Apostle. God was extremely patient with Peter even though he denied Christ three times and struggled in understanding God's direction for his life. Peter was the first Apostle to recognize Jesus as the Messiah, the first to take on the commitment to full service, and the first to lead the Apostles in forming the church. His single purpose in life was to please God, preach the gospel, serve the poor, and to lead the Apostles. The Holy Spirit over took Peter in a great way that allowed him to perform miracles, to preach a message that saved the souls of over three thousand in one meeting, and to direct the Apostles in forming the church. Peter was truly a unique individual that lived for his Savior and devoted a hundred percent of his life to saving souls.

The Jewish culture was deeply rooted in following the Jewish leadership and obeying Jewish law. Any deviation from the Jewish law was strongly discouraged and could result in stoning. King Herod and the Roman government were constantly looking for any signs of trouble within the local Jewish community for fear of a revolt against their ruthless control. When

Herod learned he would gain favor for killing James, he started an effort to punish the Apostles and jailed Peter. Herod's plan was to jail Peter and place him on display in a public trial. This would both allow the Jews to air their hatred of the Apostles and for Herod to build a good reputation among the Jews. Peter and the Apostles were forced to avoid both the Jewish and Roman leadership to prevent persecution and to stay alive.

Peter traveled to Antioch (ruins lie near Antakya, Turkey) where Christianity grew in popularity. Antioch is also known as the Cradle of Christianity.

It is believed Peter then traveled to Rome where he worked in forming the early Christian church in Rome. It is believed this was also during the time of Nero and the great fire that consumed most of Rome. Emperor Nero placed the blame for the fire on the Christians in the city and looked to jail Peter and have him put to death. The Apostle Peter in 64AD elected to be crucified upside down, since he felt he was not worthy to be crucified in the same manner as Jesus his Savior.

John 21: 5-7 reads, "Then Jesus saith unto them, children have ye any meat? They answered him, No. And he saith unto them, Cast the net on the right side of the ship, and ye shall find. They cast therefore, and now they were not able to draw it for the multitude of fishes. Therefore that disciple whom Jesus loved saith unto Peter, It is the Lord. Now when Simon Peter heard that it was the Lord, he girt his fisher's coat unto him, for he was naked, and did cast himself into the sea."

The Apostle John was involved in the miracle of catching so many fish that it almost sank the fishing boats. In fact, the Apostle John appears to be involved in most of Jesus' miracles.

The Apostle Peter at one point asked a question about the Apostle John and his future. Jesus basically tells Apostle Peter that it is not any of his concern and that he should concentrate on following Jesus' direction.

John 21: 20-23 reads, "Then Peter, turning about, seeth the disciple whom Jesus loved following; which also leaned on his bread at supper, and said, Lord, which is he that betrayeth thee? Peter seeing him saith to Jesus, Lord, and what shall this man do? Jesus saith unto him, If I will that he tarry till I come, what is that to thee? Follow thou me."

Jesus at this point gives some indication that he may have special plans for the Apostle John and his future mission. The Apostle John did live out his life to the age of ninety four at the Church of Ephesus where he continued his work preaching and writing.

The Apostle John confirms that he can testify of these facts since he was physically present with Jesus as he preached, healed the weak and died on the cross to provide all of mankind a path to salvation.

John 21:24 reads, "This is the disciple which testifieth of these things, and wrote these things: and we know that his testimony is true."

The Holy Bible only records a small portion of all that was spoken by Jesus and the many acts of passion He completed. The Apostle John guided by the Holy Spirit recorded all that needed to be transcribed and to be included in the Holy Bible.

The Apostle John was part of the inner circle of Disciples that received personal instruction from Jesus as he raised people from the dead, healed people from many different illnesses and provided the way of salvation.

Mark 5:37-40 reads, "And he suffered no man to follow him, save Peter, and James, and John the brother of James. And he cometh to the house of the ruler of the synagogue, and seeth the tumult, and them that wept and wailed greatly. And when he was come in, he saith unto them, Why make ye this ado, and weep? The damsel is not dead, but sleepeth." And they laughed him to scorn. But when he had put them all out, he taketh the father and the mother of the damsel, and them that were with him, and entereth in where the damsel was lying."

Jesus instructs John, Peter, and James that those that are disruptive, negative, and faithless need to be removed from the area. Jesus at this time purged the room, the house, and the premises of all the people that were laughing him to scorn. Our thoughts, deeds, and emotions are either righteous or sinful. People are either in the light or in the darkness. In this case, sin and Satan were in control of these people that were laughing. Each day we need to be aware of our speech, thoughts, and emotions to ensure they are not sinful.

Jesus was teaching the Apostle Peter and others you should not proceed until the area is clean of sin and those that are present are believers. This powerful and miraculous miracle occurred when Jesus was in complete control. We struggle with righteousness and sin throughout the day as we entertain ideas and thoughts, consider actions to take, and decide on language to use.

Peter was also present in the Upper Room and in the Garden of Gethsemane. It was late when the disciples left the last supper and walked through the dark streets of Jerusalem on their way to the Mount of Olives. The Apostle John had no idea that the information he just received about the betrayal from Jesus would transpire within hours at the Garden of Gethsemane. Jesus continued to teach and prepare his disciples about His betrayal, death and resurrection.

John 15: 1–7 reads, "I am the true vine, and my Father is the husbandman. Every branch in me that beareth not fruit he taketh away; and every branch that beareth fruit, he purgeth it, that it may bring forth more fruit. Now ye are clean through the word which I have spoken unto you. Abide in me, and I in you. As the branch cannot bear fruit of itself, except it abide in the vine: no more can ye, except ye abide in me. I am the vine, ye are the branches: He that abideth in me, and I in him, the same bringeth forth much fruit: for without me ye can do nothing. If a man abide not in me, he is cast forth as a branch, and is withered; and men gather them, and cast them into fire, and they are burned. If ye abide in me, and my words abide in you, ye shall ask what ye will, and it shall be done unto you."

Jesus explained to the Apostles that they were to preach the gospel and to allow the Holy Spirit to save souls. He also explains that as their understanding becomes more complete and their testimony becomes more effective He would become more involved in their lives. Jesus their Lord through the Holy Spirit guided them, he corrected them, and he open new paths for them to follow.

Jesus continued to instruct his Apostles and to ensure them that he would provide for their needs. They would need to allow the Holy Spirit to take control of their lives and direct them so that many may hear Gods' word and believe.

The Apostle Peter and the other disciples continued to walk in the dark to the Garden of Gethsemane where Jesus prayed. It was the Apostle John who listened with great care to record Jesus' prayer.

John 17: 1–26 reads, "These words spake Jesus, and lifted up his eyes to heaven, and said, "Father, the hour is come; glorify thy Son, that the Son also may glorify thee. As thou hast given him power over all flesh, that he should give eternal life to as many as thou hast given him. And this is life eternal, that they might know thee the only true God, and Jesus Christ, whom thou hast sent. I have glorified thee on the earth: I have finished the work which thou gavest me to do. And now, O Father, glorify thou me with thine own self with the glory which I had with thee before the world was. I have manifested thy name unto the men which thou gavest me out of the world: thine they were, and thou gavest them me: and they have kept thy word. Now they have know that all things whatsoever thou hast given me are of thee. For I have given unto them the words which thou gavest me; and they have received them, and have known surely that I came out from thee, and they have believed that thou didst send me. I pray for them: I pray not for the world, but for them which thou hast given me; for they are thine. And all mine are thine, and thine are mine; and I am glorified in them. And now I am no more in the world, but these are in the world, and I come to thee. Holy Father, keep through thine own name those whom thou hast given me, that they may be one, as we are. While I was with them in the world, I kept them in thy name: those that thou gavest me I have kept, and none of them is lost, but the son of perdition; that the scripture might be fulfilled. And now come I to thee; and these things I speak to the world, that they might have my joy fulfilled in themselves. I have given them thy word; and the world hath hated them, because they are not of the world, even as I am not of the world. I pray not that thou shouldest take them out of the world, but that shouldest keep them from evil. They are not of the world, even as I am not of the world. Sanctity them through thy truth; thy word is truth. As thou hast sent me into the world, even so have I also sent them into the world. And for their sakes I sanctify myself, that they also might be sanctified through the truth. Neither pray I for these alone, but for them also which shall believe on me through their word: That they all may be one; as thou, Father, art in me, and I in thee, that they also may be one in us: that the world may believe that thou hast sent me. And the glory which thou gavest me I have given them; that they may be one, even as we are one: I in them, and thou in me, that they may be made perfect in one; and that the world may know that thou hast sent me, and hast loved them, as thou hast loved me. Father, I will that they also, whom thou hast given me, be with me where I am; that they may behold my glory, which thou hast given me: for thou lovedst, me before the foundation of the world. O righteous Father, the world hath not know thee: but I have know thee, and these have know that thou hast sent me. And I have declared unto them thy name, and will declare it: that the love wherewith thou hast loved me may be in them, and I in them."

The Apostle Peter and others were in the Garden of Gethsemane with Jesus when He prayed. Jesus' prayer was to glorify God, and to benefit those present (His Apostles) and for future generations. Jesus prayed that His work was complete here on earth and that He was resting in God's will and His return to the realm of eternity.

Jesus also prayed for the Apostles and their faith, knowledge, love, and the indwelling of the Holy Spirit. As the Son, he verifies that His Apostles are no longer part of the world that hates them because of their faith in their Lord Jesus the Christ. He prays for those that will become believers by hearing the words spoken by His Apostles.

The prayer is also a request from the Son to the Father for glory to be given out so that all that hear and see may be blessed. This glory is based on the manifestation of God's gracious love of the Father for the Son and for all of mankind.

The Son was glorified by the Father by giving him authority over all of man's weaknesses. The Son glorified the Father by giving eternal life to all those who believed in the Lord Jesus Christ.

The Apostle Peter and his understanding of the glorification of the Father and the Son were based on this prayer, Jesus' life, and teachings. The relationship that was lost with the fall of man will be restored due the works completed by Jesus, His obedience, death, and resurrection.

It is believed that some of the Apostles continued to live in Jerusalem for a number of years even after the Crucifixion and Resurrection of Jesus. In about 36 AD, the persecution of Christians continued with Stephen being stoned to death for preaching the gospel. The persecution continued as the Apostle James was executed in about 44AD by King Agrippa. The Apostle John experienced a great loss with the death of his brother James and now the danger was too great for his family to live in the Promised Land settled by the twelve tribes of Judah. John rose to a position of prominence in the Christian Church and was able to move before the destruction of Jerusalem in 70AD by the Romans.

Sometime after this continued persecution of Christians the Apostles started moving to others areas outside of Israel. At this time it is believed the Apostle John moved his family (including the Mother of Jesus) to Ephesus of Asia (Turkey). He was able to move his family away from immediate danger and help spread the gospel to the West. The Apostle John continued his preaching for a number of years and worked with the Apostle Paul, the Apostle Peter, the Apostle Timothy and others in spreading the gospel throughout Asia and West to Europe. Ephesus was known as a city of learning where Christians such as the Apostle John and the Apostle Paul were able to preach the gospel to crowds gathered in the lecture halls. The ministry grew as more people witnessed the healing power of the Holy Spirit and those that were released from demons.

Ephesus was the capital of Asia Minor and the center for trade in the area. The temple of Artemis was built in Ephesus by the Greeks and attracted many worshipers from all around the area. With the worshipers of pagan gods came a great deal of money for the city of Ephesus. There were seven Christian churches in the area that Paul and John ministered to. Like Antioch and Cornith, Ephesus was a port city that allowed many of the disciples to travel between churches. It is believed that the Apostle Paul wrote many of his letters here over a period as long as three years and may have also been imprisoned in Ephesus.

Emperor Domitian realized that these worshipers of the goddess Artemis were responsible for donating a great deal of money to the Roman Government and that the new Christian Churches were discouraging more donations. The Roman Government generally considered the Christian church another cult that caused problems for the government by challenging the worship of pagan gods and all the other related businesses.

The Apostle Peter was part of the inner circle and leader of the Apostles. Peter was the Apostle that first realized who Jesus was and was anxious to make that confirmation with Jesus and the other disciples.

Matthew 16:16 reads, "And Simon Peter answered and said, Thou art the Christ, the son of the living God."

Jesus acknowledged Peter as a person that would have a major impact on building the church and would be empowered by the Holy Spirit to heal and convert both Jews and Gentiles. The church would grow in numbers as the Apostle Peter the other Apostles continued to preach the news that Jesus was the Messiah and that their salvation is free if only they believed.

Matthew 16:18–19 reads, "And I say also unto thee, That thou art Peter, and upon this rock I will build my church; and the gates of hell shall not prevail against it. And I will give unto thee the keys of the kingdom of heaven: and whatsoever thou shalt bind on earth shall be bound in heaven: and whatsoever thou shalt loose on earth shalt be loosed in heaven."

Jesus gave the Apostle Peter the keys to heaven. It was at the Day of Pentecost when the Apostle Peter first opened the door to heaven when he began to preach. The Apostle Peter was filled with the Holy Spirit and with God's authority when he began to share God's will for man and how salvation was available for all. Many that heard the Apostle's Peter's words that day believed and allowed the Holy Spirit to enter into their lives. The Apostle Peter had the privilege to announce to those who believed in the

Lord Jesus Christ that their sins were forgiven and that the doors to heaven were open for them.

Matthew 16:21–22 reads, "From that time forth began Jesus to show unto his disciples, how that he must go unto Jerusalem, and suffer many things of the elders and chief priests and scribes, and be killed, and be raised again the third day. Then Peter took him, and began to rebuke him, saying, Be it far from thee, Lord: this shall not be unto thee."

Jesus had given the Apostles by this time the faith to withstand the pain and suffering that they would endure as their Savior and Lord was crucified. However, the Apostle Peter was distressed to hear this and did not understand why Jesus' death needed to take place.

Jesus had transformed Peter from a poorly educated man with few skills as a preacher to a man with great courage and faithfulness. He became part of the inner circle of Jesus' Apostles and was present during the Transfiguration. He achieved greatness within the church and held a special position. He began as a man with very humble beginnings and was able to achieve a special position within the church because of his solid rock faith in the Lord Jesus the Christ.

Peter was headstrong and would tell people what to do. He even attempted to tell Jesus what to do. He made many mistakes and was often impetuous and would talk before thinking. He denied Christ three times, he cut off the ear of the high priest's guard, and fell asleep in the garden as Jesus prayed.

However, Peter was also blessed by Jesus and was given the authority to heal and complete miracles. He was able to cast out demons and people were healed simply by believing and being in his presence.

Acts 9: 40–43 reads, "But Peter put them all forth, and kneeled down, and prayed; and turning him to the body said, Tabitha, arise. And she opened her eyes: and when she saw Peter, she sat up. And he gave her his hand, and lifted her up, and when had called the saints and widows, presented her alive. And it was known throughout all Joppa; and many believed in the Lord. And it came to pass, that he tarred many days in Joppa with Simon a tanner."

Some of the personality traits that caused Peter many problems also worked to establish a base for greatness as a man of God.

Peter's denial of Christ haunted him and caused him to fall into complete repentance when Jesus asked him three times if he loved him. This reaffirmation allowed Peter to move from a fearful man to man of great maturity and courage. In a state of complete commitment he was able to grow in faith and benefit from a closer walk with his Lord and Savior. Peter's faith in Jesus was responsible for making a dramatic change in Peter from a fisherman to a great leader of the Christian church.

The Apostle Peter and the other Apostles were under pressure by the Roman and Jewish leadership for establishing a church that would challenge their own interests for both financial control and the leadership of the people. The Apostle Peter was eventually jailed and sentenced to death. He asked to be crucified upside down because he felt he was not worthy to be crucified in the same manner as his Lord.

We need to learn from The Apostle Peter and ask ourselves are we living a completely committed life that glorifies our Lord and Savior. As The Apostle Peter, we need to learn from our mistakes, grow in maturity, and become more courageous in our walk and in our ministry. We all make mistakes and we need to spend time in prayer to ask for forgiveness. God will transform us through the study of His word, allowing the Holy Spirit to speak to us, and to take time to recognize how the Holy Spirit works both in our lives and in the lives of others.

It was the Apostle Peter who recognized Jesus first at Galilee and could not wait for the boat and jumped into the sea to meet Jesus. It was the Apostle Peter who was the first to acknowledge Jesus as the Messiah. It was the Apostle Peter who quickly drew his sword to defend Jesus in the Garden of Gethsemane. And, it was God who sent an Angel to release the Apostle Peter from prison.

Acts 12:11 reads, "And when Peter was come to himself, he said, Now I know of a surely, that the hath sent his angel, and hath delivered me out of the hand of Herod, and from all the expectation of the people of the Jews."

Paul the Apostle

Approximately (5 AD to 67 AD)

In about 57 AD the Apostle Paul was arrested for breaking Jewish law. He was accused of defiling the temple by bringing Gentiles into it and for not teaching the laws of Moses. Later, Paul did exercise his rights as a Roman citizen and asked that he be allowed the appeal to Caesar. The Apostle Paul accompanied by a centurion was placed in chains and was transported from Caesarea to Rome by ship. The ship with 276 passengers was caught in a storm and was blown off course by six hundred miles over a two week time period that ended in a ship wreak on the island of Malta. All 276 passengers survived the storm.

Acts 27:21–23 reads, "But after a long abstinence Paul stood forth in the midst of them, and said, Sirs, ye should have hearkened unto me, and not have loosed from Crete, and to have gained this harm and loss. And now I exhort you to be of good cheer: for there shall be no loss of any man's life among you, but of the ship. For there stood by me this night the angel of God, whose I am, and whom I serve."

God heard the Apostle Paul's fervent prayers for the deliverance of the ship and all those on board. God sent an angel that stood before the Apostle Paul and explained that God would deliver him from the storm to stand in front of Caesar in Rome.

Application

The Apostle Paul was a great man of faith that God recognized and blessed. It was the Apostle Paul's fervent prayers that God answered and sent His angel to deliver His response. This angel was sent by God for a number of different reasons. God ensured Paul that his prayers were heard and that he was in God's plan. The angel also explained that the storm would end and that all would be saved. All 276 people on the ship would benefit from Paul's faith and leadership.

Paul never forgot to pray for the churches and their specific needs. In Colossians the Apostle Paul's prayer is focused on the needs within the church at Colossae.

Colossians 1: 9–12 reads, "For this cause we also, since the day we heard it, do not cease to pray for you, and to desire that ye might be filled with the knowledge of his will in all wisdom and spiritual understanding; That ye might walk worthy of the Lord unto all pleasing, being fruitful in every good work, and increasing in the knowledge of God; Strengthened with all might, according to his glorious power, unto all patience and long-suffering with joyfulness; Giving thanks unto the Father, which hath made us meet to be partakers of the inheritance of the saints in light:"

Paul's prayers included a request for a thorough understanding of God's will for all of mankind. This would include having the ability to accumulate spiritual principals found in scripture and applying them to our daily lives. Paul's daily prayers always included the needs of the church and all of the members. Specific needs for the church included strength to endure all of the challenges, patience to endure suffering, and restraint to avoid retaliation.

Our prayers need to be addressed to our God the Creator of the universe and the church. We worship God the Father and through Him alone we are dependent on Him for our salvation.

John the Apostle

Approximately (7 AD to 100 AD)

JOHN WAS HONORED BY Jesus as He hung on the cross.

John 19: 25–27 reads, "Now there stood by the cross of Jesus his mother, and his mother's sister, Mary the wife of Cleophas, and Mary Magdalene. When Jesus therefore saw his mother, and the disciples standing by, whom he loved, he saith unto his mother, Woman behold thy son! Then saith he to the disciples, Behold thy mother! And from that hour that disciple took her unto his own house."

The very last words spoken by Jesus are directed at his beloved mother and disciples. Jesus' death on the cross paid for all of man's sin. From that time forward John and the disciples ensured that Jesus' mother (Mary) would be protected and that all of her needs would be met. The danger was great with the Sanhedrin and now the Roman Government was willing to execute those that are found guilty of blasphemy. Members of the Sanhedrin were looking for all those who were associated with Jesus. Consequently, John and the Apostles went to great lengths to ensure that Jesus' mother (Mary) was protected and out of danger.

John was called the beloved Apostle by Jesus and a messenger from God. He was the youngest of the Apostles and lived a long life, and was believed to have died in Ephesus at the age of ninety four. It is generally agreed that the Apostle John was responsible for writing the Gospel of John, three Epistles of John, and Book of Revelations. It is believed he moved from Israel between 33 AD to 70 AD with his family and extended family (including Mary the mother of Jesus) to support the Apostle Paul and the churches he started in Ephesus. The Apostle Paul died about 67 AD and the Apostle Peter died about 64 AD which left the Apostle John as the oldest original Apostle living from about 64 AD to 100 AD. This placed the Apostle John in the leadership role of the Ephesus church and subject to all the responsibilities. In about 95 AD he was banished to the Island of Patmos for a period of time and evidentially returned to the church of Ephesus.

The Roman Government had increased its efforts to eliminate the Christian church by capturing its leaders and placing them in prison or charging them with some type of punishment such as banishment. The Apostle John was arrested and banished to the small island of Patmos. These small islands did have mines where criminals were forced to work under extreme conditions.

As a Son of Thunder, the Apostle John had experienced a great deal of joy and sorrow. While imprisoned on the Island of Patmos the Apostle John began to be given great insights by the Holy Spirit. He was able to record these ideas and visions that would be later become the book of Revelation. The Apostle John also had students such as Polycarp and others that studied under his direction.

It is believed that the Apostle John was eventually released from Patmos and returned to Ephesus as head of the Church of Ephesus. The Apostle John was the last of the Apostles and died in Ephesus at an age greater than 90.

John states the purpose of the book in John 20:31, which reads, "But these are written, that ye might believe that Jesus is the Christ, the son of God; and that believing ye might have life through his name." John defines the gospel clearly as either living in the light or living in the darkness. He also explains that those that are living in the darkness hate the light because it exposes their evil deeds, their evil desires, and their evil priorities.

Mark 3:17 reads, "And James the son of Zebedee, and John the brother of James; and he surnamed them Boanerges, which is, The sons of thunder:"

John and his older brother the Apostle James (James the Greater) were also called by Jesus as the Sons of Thunder. Both men had little patience and when pushed to their limits would speak out loudly and chastise people for their sinful nature.

Luke 9: 53–56 reads, "And they did not receive him, because his face was as though he would go to Jerusalem. And when his disciples James and John saw this, they said, Lord, wilt thou that we command fire to come down from heaven, and consume them, even as Elijah did? But he turned, and rebuked them, and said, Ye know not what manner of spirit ye are of. For the Son of man is not come to destroy man's lives, but to save them. And they went to another village."

However, both men were reprimanded by Jesus and they both seemed to be able keep their temper under control. The Apostle Johns' writings do at times reflect shortness with those that do not believe and are not willing to change their lives. John's writings reflected a long life that was filled with many experiences such as the crucifixion of his Lord and Savior, the death of other beloved Apostles, the death of his brother James, and the teachings of Jesus. The Apostle John's life was transformed, changing a young man with great intensity to an old man with great wisdom where faith became vision. These changes were made in spite of John's make-up. In other words Jesus is able mold a man into what he chooses regardless of past experiences.

The Apostle John was a student that sat at the feet of his Master for three years, absorbing as much as humanly possible. He watched and experienced the washing of his feet by his Lord and Savior, Jesus. This simple act had a profound impact on John's understanding of what it meant to be a servant of the Lord. The fact that Jesus (God's only Son) would wash his feet, a task for a lowly servant, was difficult to understand, extremely humbling, and unbelievable. John was learning that we are servants to the gospel and that it is our mission in this life is to teach and preach the saving grace of God's word throughout the world. John grew to be a man of great passion, humility, and at the same time a man of great courage.

The Apostle John's life on the Island of Patmos was similar to that of Elijah. He lived in a cave where he was cut off from the outside world and was able to commune with his Lord and Savior. Both John and Elijah received prophetic revelations from God in this state where both men were being persecuted for preaching God's word. It was John being brandished to the Island of Patmos that allowed John to write the Book of Revelation.

Revelation 1:9 reads, "I John, who also am your brother, and companion in tribulation, and in the kingdom and patience of Jesus Christ, was in the isle that is called Patmos, for the word of god, and for the testimony of Jesus Christ."

The instruction John received from Jesus allowed him to serve his time on Patmos with an attitude of servitude, patience, and endurance knowing that his earthly experience would be met with grace and the glory of his heavenly Father.

The Apostle John was called the Beloved Apostle by Jesus. The Apostle John was passionate about the true word of God and how it affected all of God's creation. He was concerned about man's relationship with his

Heavenly Father and the need to love your neighbor, to be obedient God's word, and to be forgiving.

1 John 1:1–3 reads, "That which was from the beginning, which we have heard, which we have seen with our eyes, which we have looked upon, and our hands have handled, of the Word of Life. For the life was manifested, and we have we have seen it, and bear witness, and show unto you that eternal life, which was with the Father, and was manifested unto us. That which we have seen and heard declare we unto you, that ye also may have fellowship with us: and truly our fellowship is with the Father, and with his Son Jesus Christ."

The Apostle John was taught by Jesus, traveled and ate with Jesus, and was present when Jesus healed the sick, raised the dead, and cast out demons. He was witness to thousands being converted from a life of sin and death to a life full of eternal grace. These experiences changed the Apostle John in many ways. He became a person with a positive attitude, his focus was on others, and he was passionate about sharing God's truth with all of mankind regardless of the risks.

Ephesians 4:15 reads, "But speaking the truth in love, may grow up into him in all things, which is the head even Christ."

The Apostle John grew to be a man that spoke the word of God in love. God's words are spoken with the purpose of turning a life away from sin to a life of Grace. God's words are spoken in confidence, with grace, humility, and compassion. There is no room for pride, boasting, or self. When we see and hear the braggart, the boaster, the know it all, it is difficult to see anything beyond that lack of respect. We are to encourage one another to develop their gifts so that the church may grow and all may share in those gifts. The church is a living functioning body that is dependent on each member to engage and contribute their gifts.

The Apostle John was also aware of rejection by family and friends. The Apostles traveled with Jesus to Nazareth where he spent his childhood and spoke in the synagogue. Jesus read from Isaiah and explained that he was the Messiah.

Isaiah 61:1 reads, "The spirit of the Lord God is upon me; because the Lord hath anointed me to preach good tidings unto the meek; he hath sent me to bind up the broken hearted, to proclaim liberty to the captives, and the opening of the prison to them that are bound."

The family and friends of Jesus could only see that Jesus was the son of a carpenter and nothing more. They became offended by what Jesus was saying and forced him to leave the synagogue and Nazareth. Family dynamics are complex and involve a history of attitudes, opinions, and experiences. It is not uncommon for family members to resist or acknowledge success or changes made by another member. Some of these difficulties are psychosomatic and some are simply a refusal to acknowledge that sin exists and they need to consider allowing Jesus to resolve their many problems. The Apostle John was able to gain a deeper understanding from Jesus of the pain and anguish that one experiences when family and friends do not accept the gospel and the saving grace of the Lord Jesus.

The Apostle John was the head of the church of Ephesus for about thirty years. During this time The Roman Empire ruled the Mediterranean area with an iron fist. Any type of revolt or unrest was met with severe punishment by either death or imprisonment that resulted in thousands of Jews being slaughtered or being enslaved and sent to Rome. The Christians during this time were considered a cult that was responsible for unrest and conflicts with the Jews. Many of the people were highly superstitious and worshiped pagan gods and blamed the Christians for any hardship. In 64 AD the Christians were blamed for the great fire in Rome and as a result many were burned or put to death. In spite of all the persecution, the church grew during this thirty year period of time that the Apostle John was head of the church. It has been estimated that 28% of the people in the area had heard God's word and it was preached in 6 different languages.

Ephesus was at that time the fourth greatest city in the region behind Rome, Alexandra, and Antioch. There was a massive temple built for the pagan goddess Diana (four times larger than the Parthenon) in Ephesus that drew thousands from around the region for all to worship for the promise of fertility, long life, and protection during child birth. Many celebrations were also held with music, dancing, singing and chanting. Many other temples and statues were also built for the pagan gods (i.e., Zeus, Apollo) for all to worship. The location of Ephesus and the temples created an economy based on worshiping of pagan gods. This economy involved trade, banking, collecting sacrificial funds for the gods, printing of money, prostitution, and other support businesses. The temple was administered by chief Priests and hundreds of other priests in support positions. It was to the financial benefit of the Roman Government to maintain and encourage the worship of the pagan gods.

The people that lived in and travel through Ephesus were polytheists and would worship many different pagan gods. They worshiped different pagan gods for different reasons (i.e., knowledge, wealth, and pleasure). The Apostle Paul, The Apostle John, The Apostle Timothy, and others had many challenges considering that the city of Ephesus had a society that was based on years of worship of pagan gods, a government that had financial interest in collecting funds at pagan temples, and that many people were very superstitious.

The Apostle John was living in a dangerous city where anyone could submit a complaint if they felt their livelihood was being threatened; someone was not showing respect to the mother goddess Diana, or claiming another god was more important than Ephesus' Goddess Diana. However, it is believed that the Jews were allowed citizenship and granted the freedom to practice their religious traditions. Paul and John did speak at the Jewish synagogue and at other locations around the Ephesus.

It was the Apostle John's ministry to encourage the Gentile Christians to realize the importance of their heavenly origin and their future with their Creator, but also to realize the responsibility to live a life on earth as those chosen of God and sealed by the Holy Spirit.

The Apostle John was a man of truth and taught the truth from the beginning for the purpose that all could have fellowship with The Holy Spirit, The Son and with The Father.

John 1:1–3 reads, "The beginning was the Word, and the Word was with God, and the Word was God. The same was in the beginning with God. All things were made by him; and without him was not any thing made that was made."

It was John's ministry that focused on the building up of the Gentiles and teaching them the law. The Apostle John's love for the church of Ephesus was repeated throughout his writings.

Revelations 2:1–3 reads, "Unto the angels of the church of Ephesus write; These things saith he that holdeth the seven stars in his right hand, who walketh in the midst of the seven golden candlesticks; I know thy works, and thy labor, and thy patience, and how thou canst not bear them which are evil: and thou hast tried them which say they are apostles, and are not, and hast found them liars. And hast borne, and hast patience, and for my names sake hast labored, and hast not fainted."

John's letter to the church was for the purpose of encouragement and love as they struggled to survive in a hostile environment where Christians were persecuted for any number of reasons. They were no longer strangers and foreigners, but they were now members of God's great kingdom of blessings that cannot be measured.

The Apostle John was persistently faithful throughout his entire life. It was Peter and John that ran together to the sepulcher the morning of the resurrection. The Apostle John experienced a great deal in his life. John changed because he had three years of training with his Savior and Lord; experienced the death and resurrection of his Savior and Lord, and saw Him later in His risen body. He experienced the death of his brother James and the death and beating of many more Apostles and early Christians. John's temperament grew to be one of great love and understanding. He was thoughtful and was able to sense God's will in each situation. John was a trusted Apostle that could be counted on and would be loved by all. It was John's love for the Church of Ephesus that caused his concern for all the members.

1 John 5:21 reads, "Little children keep yourselves from idols. Amen."

The pagan life in Ephesus was permeated with idols in virtually every aspect of daily life. It was only through the power of the Holy Spirit that these first converts to Christianity were able to separate themselves from pagan life and learn how to love others and obey God's commandments. It is only at that point when a true understanding of God's will is realized that a fervent love for others and a love for obedience began to grow.

The Apostle John and his life's work was always centered on the truth and the fruit of the Holy Spirit and love.

John 3:16 reads, "For God so loved the world, that he gave his only begotten Son, that whosoever believeth in him should not perish, but have everlasting life."

John 14:15 reads, "If ye love me, keep my commandments."

1 John 3:10–11 reads, "In this the children of God are manifest, and the children of the devil: whosoever doeth not righteousness is not of God, nether he that loveth not his brother. For this is the message that ye heard from the beginning, that we should love one another."

1 John 4:7–12 reads, "Beloved, let us love one another: for love is of God; and everyone that loveth is born of God, and knoweth God. He that loveth not knoweth not God; for God is love. In this was manifested the love of God toward us, because that God sent his only begotten Son into the world, that we might live through him. Herein is love, not that we loved God, but that he loved us, and sent his Son to be the propitiation for our sin. Beloved, if God so loved us, we ought also to love one another. No man

hath seen God at any time. If we love one another, God dwelleth in us, and his love is perfected in us."

1 John 4:17-19 reads, "Herein is our love made perfect, that we may have boldness in the day of judgment: because as he is, so are we in this world. There is no fear in love; but perfect love casteth out fear: because fear hath torment. He that feareth is not made perfect in love. We love him, because he first loved us."

1 John 5:2-3 reads, "By this we know that we love the children of God, when we love God, and keep his commandments. For this is the love of God, that we keep his commandments: and his commandments are not grievous."

More than any other disciple the Apostle John spoke and wrote about loving your neighbor and following the commandments.

Matthew 22: 37-40 reads, "Jesus said unto him, Thou shalt love Lord thy God with all thy heart, and with all thy soul, and with all thy mind. This is the first and great commandment. And the second is like unto it, thou shalt love thy neighbor as thyself. On these two commandments hang all the law and the prophets."

The Apostle John was following Jesus' teachings that loving the Lord God with all your heart, soul and mind is paramount for a person to begin a personal relationship with their Creator. This is a natural desire that God has placed within each person that cannot be filled by any accomplishment, possession, and any amount of wealth. The Holy Spirit will change each person that is willing to open their heart, soul, and mind and will convict them of the need to obey God's commandments.

The Apostle John spent his entire adult life teaching about God's love for His creation. The people of Ephesus were lost in a culture that worshiped stone idols in the hope that they would receive a better life. They had hundreds of priests that were well versed on mythology and would tell them about the many pagan gods and goddesses. However, there was no one that knew about Jesus Christ and the saving grace that was available to all of mankind. There was no one that knew that the Creator of all mankind sacrificed His Only Son so that all of mankind may be allowed access to life everlasting. There was no one that knew that the greatest commandment was to love God with all your heart, with your soul, and with all your mind. And, to love your neighbor as you would love yourself. Obviously, the Apostle John and the Church of Ephesus had the tremendous challenge to preach the message of the gospel under the continual threat of persecution and possible death.

The Ephesus church and the other churches in the area were struggling with people that knew only of the pagan gods that they had always worshiped. They were worshiping these pagan gods hoping their needs for food, shelter, pleasure, greed, wealth, envy, and others would be met. There was pagan gods for every need including acts of perversion, satanic, and debauchery. There were few or no moral standards and the people were only subject to Roman Laws and the opinions of priests at the Ephesus' temples.

A pagan god is anything that prevents you from worshiping our Lord and Savior. Anything that takes priority or prevents you from worshiping our Lord and Savior is a pagan god. The people of today as the people of Ephesus are focused on self and experiencing as much pleasure as possible. The church is no longer a priority.

In Europe today you see many grand magnificent churches that are no longer used as churches. They are in many cases being maintained and managed by different governments. In some cases they are being destroyed or being used for other purposes rather than for worship. These churches were built by thousands of saints that sacrificed a great deal of time and money so that many generations may have a place to worship their Creator.

The Apostle John was able to write the Book of Revelation with divine intervention from God. At the age of ninety two John was imprisoned on the Island of Patmos. This remote island in the Aegean Sea was used by the Romans as a prison for political and religious prisoners and for mining. John's crime was his continual preaching of Jesus' saving Grace to those in Ephesus.

Revelation 1:1 reads, "The Revelation of Jesus Christ, which God gave unto him, to show unto his servants things which must shortly come to pass; and he sent and signified it by his angel unto his servant John."

God's messenger an angel was sent to John for the purpose of documenting the word of God. The book reveals God plan for mankind centered around God's only Son, Jesus Christ.

John's relationship with God's angel of interpretation was over a period of time to complete the Book of Revelation. At one point John begins to worship this angel and is quickly told to stop by the angel.

Revelation 19:10 reads, "And I fell at his feet to worship him. And he said unto me, See thou do it not: I am thy fellow servant, and of thy brethren that have the testimony of Jesus: worship God: for the testimony of Jesus is the spirit of prophecy."

We are commanded to only worship God. All of all our possessions, experiences, achievements and our very breath were given to us by God and belong to Him.

Application

Unfortunately, today many churches are no longer attended due to a generation of people that are no longer interested in religion. Many of the younger generation of today have fallen prey to the same temptations that all men have fallen to since the beginning of time. They are focused on self and the worship of wealth, pleasure, status and anything that will satisfy their greed. These are the same issues that Moses, Elijah, Peter, James, and John had to deal with. Pagan gods have always been a temptation for man since they appeal to man's greed and sense of self.

The basic mission of the Apostle John as well as other saints was to minister to all of man that their Creator loved them and had provided a way for their salvation through his Son, Jesus the Christ. In addition, God was patiently waiting for them to realize that they needed to worship the all powerful, all knowing God, ever present God; their Creator.

The Apostle John was a loving and compassionate man that spent his life serving God's people and ministering the message of salvation to the world. It is believed that during his last years he was carried to church so that he may worship with the people of the church of Ephesus. It is believed that his last words were; children love one another.

The brothers (Apostle John, Apostle James) had little patience with the Samaritans and were enraged that this village did not welcome Jesus. They wanted the wrath of God to destroy the entire village and its people. These were not men that would understand or appreciate what is transpiring in some churches today. The "feel good" church of today makes it easy to be a Christian since nothing is taught about sin and repentance. Sin is not defined and people are lead to believe they can continue living a life that is consumed in striving for more wealth, for more material possessions, and for some higher status in the community. You see no love in their lives, no peace, and no love for others. Their focus is entirely on themselves and what they can gain or steal from others. They are like leaches on society that have no purpose other than to suck the life out of others.

1 John 3:7 reads, "Little children, let no man deceive you: he that doeth righteousness is righteous, even as he is righteous."

Sin is of Satan and has no place in the church. The church in many situations no longer teaches about what is the real purpose of life and what is required of man on a daily basis. Jesus and disciples were persecuted and martyred because they spoke of sin and challenged the Jews to accept Jesus as their Messiah.

Matthew 7:13–14 reads, "Enter ye in at the strait gate: for wide is the gate, and broad is the way, that leadeth to destruction, and many there be, which go in thereat. Because strait is the gate, and narrow is the way, which leadeth unto life, and few there be that find it."

The gate to eternal life is narrow and Jesus is the gate that one must pass through to find God's grace and salvation.

Jesus corrected the Apostle John and the Apostle James and told them that he would not destroy the village because he came to save lives and not to destroy them. Jesus again showed his love and patience for the Samaritans and allowed them more time to make a decision of commitment to Christianity.

We need to be careful not to rush to judgment of others. God has a plan for each and every man and only He will make the final judgment. However, we should run from evil and not entertain evil practices and ideas.

Proverbs 3: 5–7 reads, "Trust in the Lord with all thine heart; and lean not unto thine own understanding. In all thine ways acknowledge him, and he shall direct thy paths. Be not wise in thine own eyes: fear the Lord, and depart from evil."

Jesus knew that His time was growing short and during the last supper He began to prepare the disciples for the betrayal, arrest, death and resurrection.

It was John the Evangelist that was seated next to Jesus and it was John who heard Jesus say who it was who betrayed Him. John was part of the inner circle of Apostles that Jesus trusted and loved. In this situation, Jesus confided only in John because he knew that some of the other Apostles could strike out in anger. For example, Peter was emotional, carried a sword and could act impetuously.

The Apostle John had a long and fruitful life that reached great heights of joy and great depths of despair. He had rejoiced with thousands when they made their decisions to believe that Jesus Christ was the Messiah. He had seen thousands realize they no longer needed to carry the weight of sin since God paid the price with the sacrifice of his only Son Jesus.

He was identified as John the Evangelist and was called the "Beloved Disciple" by Jesus. It is believed that it was the Apostle John who stood next to Mary when Jesus hung on the cross and it was the Apostle John that cared for Mary as his mother from that time forward. It was John who Jesus confided in during the last supper and spoke of his betrayer. John understood the message of loving your neighbor and treating others as you wish to be treated.

The Apostle John was a faithful student of Jesus and spent most of his adult life preaching to those who were lost to their own sense of self, recording the life of Jesus, and explaining man's relationship to his Father in heaven. John was practical in his approach to teaching the gospel and spent a great deal of time explaining the dangers that face all of mankind. He warned of false teachers and encouraged believers to be obedient to God's commands.

In the book of Revelation, the Apostle John speaks of the conflict between God and Satan and the prevailing victory by God. The Apostle John's writings were directed at the churches in Ephesus and to encourage those that were being persecuted. The Roman Empire and its leaders had destroyed Jerusalem and killed thousands of Jews and were continuing to execute Christians when it was in their best interest.

The Apostle John encouraged the Christian church and it's believers to hold fast to their belief and faith in their Lord and Savior. The persecution of Christians will continue as long as Satan is able to control and influence men's hearts and minds.

As Christians we live a life that is protected by God and his angels. We can take comfort in knowing no matter how difficult the situation God is always in control and He is our protector from all evil. God at any time can send down His angels to guard us from any evil that we may encounter.

Angels are spoken of throughout the Bible in many different situations and for many different purposes.

Psalm 91:11 reads, "For he shall give his angels charge over thee, to keep thee in all thy ways."

Christians that are faithful and diligent in living a righteous life are carefully cared for by God and His angels.

Psalm 34:7 reads, "The angel of the Lord encampeth round about them that fear him, and delivereth them."

God's Messengers

Christians are also careful to thank God for each of his many blessings. They are also careful to give all their praise to God for His continued protection. Angels are servants of God and are involved in communicating and delivering God's blessings and protection to the faithful each day.

Both the angels and mankind were given free will and the freedom to choose to love God or to reject Him. Loving God involves following God's commands and worshiping Him always or to deny Him, refuse to follow His commands and refuse the gift of His only Son.

James the Apostle

Approximately (3 AD to 44 AD)

THE APOSTLE JAMES (JAMES the Greater) was another one chosen by Jesus to be a messenger of God's word. Jesus referred to James and John as the sons of thunder for their strong character and at times their quick temper. James was the older brother of John and took that responsibility with great importance. It is believed that James did spend years in Spain preaching the gospel. He knew Jesus and knew He was who He said He was. Soon after the ascension of The Lord Jesus Christ, James was filled with the Holy Spirit and preached with the Holy Spirit's direction to the people of Jerusalem, Samaria, and Judaea. His preaching was heard both by the Jews and the Samaritans. James, Peter, and John were present when Jesus raised Jairus's daughter back from death. They were the prominent and chosen Apostles and were present at the Agony of Gethsemane.

The Apostle James had a burning evangelical zeal for the gospel and preached to many in Israel and possibly Spain. His preaching was fearless, loud, forceful, effective, and he soon developed a reputation with the Jewish Synagogues. He was challenging the Jewish leadership, their laws and beliefs and caused them to conspire with the Romans to have him silenced.

It is believed it was James' fiery preaching that helped to ignite the spread of the gospel throughout Israel and possibly in Spain. The Apostle James was a threat to the Jewish leadership and a problem for the Roman leadership. The Apostle James continually repeated that Jesus was the true Messiah and the Savior of the world. It was James and John who said yes to Jesus when he asked can you drink from the cup.

Mark 10:38 reads, "But Jesus said unto them, Ye know not what ye ask: can ye drink of the cup that I drink of? And be baptized with the baptism that I am baptized with?"

The Apostle James knew what drinking the cup meant and He wanted to give his life for the sake of the gospel. He lived his life for one purpose and that one purpose was to preach the saving grace of the Lord Jesus Christ. As the Apostle James walked to his death, he was preaching the gospel of Christ and spoke of his joy to serve His Savior and Lord, the Messiah.

It had been about ten years since the Crucifixion of Jesus, and the death of the Apostle James would have had a traumatic impact on the Apostles. The death would have brought back the severe anguish and confusion when Jesus hung on the cross. They were reminded that their lives were in danger and especially now that King Herod realized that James' death curried favor from the Jews.

As Moses and Elijah, the Apostle James was a man of great courage. With God's blessing and the indwelling of the Holy Spirit, the Apostle James spoke fearlessly with great zeal that resulted in the conversion of many Jews. His message was clear then and today, God is calling all men to change their lives, to believe in Jesus, to run from evil, to ask for forgiveness, and to love your neighbor.

Application

Today we need to renounce our many selfish desires and eliminate any selfish pursuit that is preventing a closer relationship with our Lord and Creator. We are followers of Jesus and are following His example that was devoted to helping others that are in need and to share the gospel of grace to those that have ears to hear. There are people waiting to hear you speak and to share your testimony so they too may rejoice as the Apostle James. As the Apostle James, we need to be willing to drink the cup, which means to share His suffering and death and love, and to give ourselves in the service of others. We are able to drink the cup because Jesus went before us and showed us the way that we too will experience the joy, the blessings, and life everlasting.

The Apostle James as the older brother of the Apostle John was a man of God and the first Apostle to be martyred. Jesus loved the Apostle James for his zeal, his fearlessness, his courage, and his impact on the conversion of the Jews and the Gentiles.

Mary Magdalene

Approximately (22 AD to 80 AD)

It was the Apostle John and the Apostle Peter that first heard the news of Jesus' resurrection from Mary Magdalene.

John 20:1–4 reads, "The first day of the week cometh Mary Magdalene early, when it was yet dark, unto the sepulcher, and seeth the stone taken away from the sepulcher. Then she runneth, and cometh to Simon Peter, and to the other disciple, whom Jesus loved, and saith unto them, They have taken away the Lord out of the sepulcher, and we know not where they have laid him. Peter therefore went forth, and the other disciple, and came to the sepulcher. So they ran both together: and the other disciple did outrun Peter, and came first to the sepulcher."

It was the Apostle John who out ran the Apostle Peter to the sepulcher to see the empty tomb.

Mary Magdalene stood outside the sepulcher weeping thinking someone had taken the body of Jesus.

John 20:11–16 reads, "But Mary stood without at the sepulcher weeping: and as she wept she stooped down, and looked into the sepulcher. And seeth two angels in white sitting, the one at the head, and the other at the feet, where the body of Jesus had lain. And they say unto her, Women, why weepest thou? She saith unto them, Because they have taken away my Lord, and I know not where they have laid him. And when she had thus said, she turned herself back, and saw Jesus standing, and knew not that it was Jesus. Jesus saith unto her, Women, why weepest thou? whom sleekest thou? She, supposed him to be the gardener, saith unto him, Sir, if thou have borne him hence, tell me where thou hast laid him, and I will take him away. Jesus saith unto her, Mary. She turned herself, and saith unto him, Rabboni; which is to say, Master."

Both the angels and Jesus spoke directly to Mary Magdalene and asked her why she was weeping. The day before, Mary Magdalene and others had watched as Jesus was beaten and scourged carrying his cross through the streets of Jerusalem and then spending three hours hanging on the cross before dying. The questions from Jesus and the angel almost seemed rhetorical since the answer was obvious. Mary Magdalene thought the body was stolen. The questions may have been designed to make Mary realize that God was in control and He would decide where Jesus' body would be placed.

The next statement made by Jesus to Mary Magdalene was that Mary Magdalene was not to hold on to him. Mary Magdalene is trying to prevent Jesus from leaving.

John 20:17 reads, "Jesus saith unto her, Touch me not; for I am not yet ascended to my Father: but go to my brethren, and say unto them, I ascend unto my Father, and your Father; and to my God, and your God."

Application

We are all focused upon our daily lives and the tasks that need to be completed. Many have grown to be extremely independent and rely on no one for support when confronted by difficulties. Many have developed strong defensive personality traits that are deployed when encountering difficult situations. The Christian has come to the realization that God is in control and that our first reaction to a difficult situation is prayer. A Christian shares many of life's difficulties and challenges with God in daily prayer and patiently waits for God's answer. The answer to difficult problems may come in many different ways and from many different sources. In some cases the answer is clear and in others cases the answer may be difficult to understand. Christians continually encourage each other to pray and ask God for all of their needs and desires.

Luke 11:9–10 reads, "And I say unto you, Ask, and it shall be given you; seek, and ye shall find; knock, and it shall be open unto you."

God's answer to prayers will be dependent on many different situations. First, God will not answer a Christian's prayer that will result in bringing harm to the Christian or those in his family. Just as parents are not willing to give their children harmful gifts, God will not give harmful gifts to Christians. Prayers are often made without a complete understanding of all those that may be effected by the request. Secondly, God knows the heart of each Christian and knows the motives behind each prayer and will respond accordingly. Another issue that may affect the answering of a prayer request may be the degree of obedience to God's commandments and statutes. There are many people that live each day in sin and refuse to admit they are living in sin.

Jesus was asked the question which commandment was the most important. Jesus' answer was to love God with all your heart, soul, and mind. He also said to love your neighbor as yourself, and to obey all of God's commandments and statutes.

Matthew 22:35-40 reads, "Then one of them, which was a lawyer, asked him a question, temping him, and saying, Master, which is the great commandment in the law? Jesus said unto him, thou shalt love the Lord God with all thy heart, and with all thy soul, and with all thy mind. This is the first and great commandment. And the second is like unto it, thou shalt love thy neighbor as thyself. On these two commandments hang all the law and the prophets."

There is obviously a direct relationship between the loving Almighty God and obeying His commandments. A Christian obeys God's commandments out of joy and not as an obedient slave. A Christian looks for opportunities to be obedient and enjoys the blessings of God's grace and peace. Today, man with Satan's support has twisted this simple principal into the idea that God created a fallen man that cannot obey God's commandments. God loves His creation and all of mankind. God gave His all, His only Son, that all who believe in Him will have eternal life. God not only gave His only Son he also gave us His word for study and direction.

The consequence for not accepting God's love and not obeying His commandments are incomprehensible.

Proverbs 28:9 reads, "He that turneth away his ear from hearing the law, even his prayer shall be abomination."

A Christian who breaks God's law will hinder the Holy Spirit that lives within him. The Holy Spirit requires a healthy mind and soul in order to convey and interpret our prayers to God.

Mary Magdalene spoke directly with Jesus and angels. Angels are God's spiritual messengers that continually convey God's messages to man. Mary may have been inconsolable and needed Jesus to reassure her that he would be raised up to heaven by His Father. God is always present and will meet the needs of each believer.

God's Messengers

John 14:6 reads, "Jesus saith unto him, I am the way, the truth, and the life: no man cometh unto the Father, but by me."

The resurrection and the defeat of death by Jesus was a momentous event that was greeted with great joy in heaven. In this single event Jesus made it possible for all believers to spend eternity in heaven.

Birth of Jesus

GOD'S ANGELS WERE THE messengers that delivered the joyous news of the birth of Jesus. The appearance of the first angel was a terrifying experience for the shepherds.

Luke 2:8–14 reads, "And there were in the same country shepherds abiding in the field, keeping watch over their flock by night. And, Lo, the angel of the Lord came upon them, and the glory of the Lord shone round about them: and they were sore afraid. And the angel said unto them, Fear not: for, behold, I bring you good tiding of great joy, which shall be to all people. For unto you is born this day in the city of David a Savior, which is Christ the Lord. And this shall be a sign unto you: Ye shall find the babe wrapped in swaddling clothes, lying in a manger. And suddenly there was with the angel a multitude of the heavenly host praising God, and saying, Glory to God in the highest, and on earth peace, good will toward men."

A great celebration took place as an army of angels raised their voices in joy over the birth of God's Son. The sky was filled with countless numbers of angels singing praises to God. This must have been an overwhelming experience for the shepherds. After the shepherds regained their composure they told others of what they had seen and traveled to the manger to worship their Savior and Lord.

The birth of Jesus was prophesied hundreds of years prior to the actual birth in Bethlehem.

Isaiah 9:6 reads, "For unto us a child is born, unto us a son is given: and the government shall be upon his shoulder: and his name shall be called Wonderful, Counselor, The mighty God, The everlasting Father, The Prince of Peace."

Application

Angels did appear before many for the purpose of delivering an important message about God's plan. A great celebration was taking place in heaven with God's Son being born in Bethlehem. This birth was the greatest gift man would ever receive. This birth would allow man to receive life everlasting through faith in Jesus Christ. Great joy and love was given to all of mankind. Countless numbers of angels were singing and praising God for His love and the birth of His Son.

We share this great joy and love with all those who are open to hearing God's word.

Mark 1:14-15 reads, "Now after that John was put in prison, Jesus came into Galilee, preaching the gospel of the kingdom of God. And saying, The time is fulfilled, and the kingdom of God is at hand: repent ye, and believe the gospel."

Jesus began his ministry in Galilee by telling all of humanity to repent from all of their sin and believe and place all of their trust in Him and His message. Sometime later Jesus taught all of humanity to pray.

Matthew 6:9-13 reads, "After this manner therefore pray ye: Our Father which art in heaven, Hallowed be thy name. Thy kingdom come. Thy will be done in earth, as it is in heaven. Give us this day our daily bread. And forgive us our debts, as we forgive our debtors. And lead us not into temptation, but deliver us from evil: For thine is the kingdom, and the power, and the glory, for ever, Amen."

Jesus' message is clear that His kingdom is near and humanity needs to be prepared. All of man's prayers are submitted for the honor and glory of God. These prayers are to conform to His plans and will. God is in control and He will not tempt us more than what we are able to handle. He knows our every thought and knows what we need. The confession of sin and the asking of forgiveness is a daily requirement for all of humanity. Those that refuse to forgive the sins committed by others against them may experience God withholding His forgiveness. In other words, how we treat others will be reflected in how God blesses us.

Testing of Jesus

THE TESTING OF JESUS was a message to all of mankind that Jesus knows and has experienced all the tests and trials that mankind will ever encounter. Jesus was God and fully man. He was tested for the purpose of being prepared by God as the perfect sacrifice in washing away the sins of the world.

After the baptism of Jesus, the Holy Spirit led Jesus in to the wilderness for forty days and nights. It was during this time that the devil tempted Jesus and tested Him by offering great wealth if He would worship Satan.

Matthew 4:11 reads, "Then the devil leaveth him, and, behold, angels came and ministered unto him."

Satan was allowed to test Jesus and place Him in difficult situations. This treatment by Satan was intense and involved three attempts to make Jesus use His divine powers.

Angels did comfort Jesus by providing peace and resolved many issues that needed attention.

Application

God is in control and will at times allow Satan to test us or may allow some other evil into our lives. Man is often tempted by the world and may live a life that is not Christ centered. Prayer and study of the Bible will open the doors to spiritual strength that will defeat the world's temptations of pride, greed and lust.

Psalm 91:11 reads, "For he shall give his angels charge over thee, to keep thee in all thy ways."

Luke 4:10 reads, "For it is written, He shall give His angels charge over thee, to keep thee."

God's Messengers

Angels are part of the believer's life and are always present to provide protection and comfort. Our daily lives as Christians are often confronted by evil and those who perpetuate evil.

We do not know the mind of God nor do we understand why he allows certain things to enter into our lives. However, we do know God is a loving, merciful, and a jealous God. He is all powerful and is able to pour out great blessings or unleash great torment. He is a just God who will not allow you to experience more temptation then you are able to handle. We trust in a God who is omnipotent, omniscient, omnipresent and we rely on His great wisdom and direction.

Exodus 23:20 reads, "Behold, I send an angel before thee, to keep thee in the way, and to bring thee into the place which I have prepared."

Hebrews 1:14 reads, "Are they not all ministering spirits, sent forth to minister for them who shall be heirs of salvation."

Man is the center of God's creation and he will be crowned with the honor and glory of salvation. We are on a journey throughout our lifetime that will include a number of tests, experiences and blessings that will prepare us to meet our Lord and Creator.

Garden of Gethsemane

THE GARDEN OF GETHSEMANE is the place where Jesus prayed before being arrested, tried, and crucified. Jesus was both God and fully man. In this garden Jesus reveals his humanity as he expresses His fear and asks God that this cup would be removed from Him. However, after an evening of prayer Jesus ultimately becomes obedient to God's word and submits to God's will.

As Jesus prayed in the Garden of Gethsemane an angel appeared for the purpose of comforting Him.

Luke 22:42–44 reads, "Saying, Father, if thou be willing, remove this cup from me: nevertheless not my will, but thine, be done. And there appeared an angel unto him from heaven, strengthening him. And being in an agony he prayed more earnestly: and his sweat was as it were great drops of blood falling down to the ground."

Jesus spent that night in prayer and taking on the sins of the world. He was God's ultimate sacrifice for all of man's sin and needed to prepare himself to carry all of man's sin to the cross.

Application

The message is that God knows our fears as part of the human race and will provide comfort and solace with our Father in a time of pain and suffering. Jesus knows the pain from betrayal as a kiss by Judas. Jesus knows the feelings of disappointment when He discovered friends had not kept watch, but had fallen asleep.

Jesus' reaction to those who arrested him was nonviolent even though He was completely innocent of any wrong doing. Jesus even healed the ear of Malchus when it was cut off by Peter with his razor sharp sword. Jesus was our living sacrifice which was offered by the Father as a payment for all the sins of mankind.

It is believed that angels are able to easily transition from the spiritual life to man's life on today's earth. In addition, man can be comforted by the Holy Spirit that lives within their earthly bodies and angels. Angels are God's messengers and their sole purpose is to reflect His continue love for all of mankind.

Luke 16:22 reads, "And it came to pass, that the beggar died, and was carried by the angels into Abraham's bosom: the rich man also died, and was buried."

Angels are with us throughout this life and will carry us to our Lord and Savior at the end of this life. God lives within us through His Holy Spirit and has adopted us into His family.

Death of Jesus

Approximately (30 AD to 33 AD)

The Sanhedrin arrested, tried, and condemned Jesus for healing on the Sabbath, threatening to destroy the Jewish Temple, using sorcery, and claiming to be the Son of God. Jesus was then taken to Pontius Pilate to be condemned for claiming to be King of the Jews. Pilate tries to release Jesus by providing another prisoner named Barabbas to take his place. The crowd insisted on having Jesus crucified.

Jesus could of had countless numbers of angels come to destroy His enemies and carry him to heaven. However, the fact is that there is a cost related to sin and Jesus was going to pay the cost for all the sins of mankind. There was no other way to pay for man's sins except a perfect sacrifice had to be made and that was the sinless life of Jesus.

God's angels were there prepared to act if needed. They were there in the Garden of Gethsemane to comfort and prepare Jesus for the crucifixion. They were at the tomb to roll away the stone and to explain to the Apostles and family what had happened to Jesus.

Luke 24:4–7 reads, "And it came to pass, as they were much perplexed thereabout, behold, two men stood by them in shining garments: And as they were afraid, and bowed down their faces to the earth, they said unto them, Why seek ye the living among the dead? He is not here, but is risen: remember how he spake unto you when he was yet in Galilee, Saying, The Son of man must be delivered into the hands of sinful men, and be crucified, and the third day rise again."

Application

Man has been involved in sin since the beginning with Adam and Eve. God has blessed man and gave him free will and power over the things of the earth. Free will opened the doors and allowed man to freely choose between love and hate. Those who love God will freely follow his commands and show that love to others.

The cross is the door that opens to heaven. A man that comes to the cross will realize Jesus paid the price for all of man's sins and that He is waiting to welcome him to eternity.

The cross is there for all of mankind. Jesus' death on the cross and His resurrection triumphed over all evil and death. No matter how difficult the situation Jesus is standing at the door waiting to welcome all who have confessed their sins and believe to heaven.

1 John 1:9 reads, "If we confess our sins, he is faithful and just to forgive us our sins, and to cleanse us from all unrighteousness."

Resurrection of Jesus

Approximately (30 AD to 33 AD)

ANGELS WERE PRESENT WITH the disciples when Jesus ascended into heaven.

Acts 1:9–11 reads, "And when he had spoken these things, while they beheld, he was taken up; and a cloud received him out of their sight. And while they looked steadfastly toward heaven as he went up, behold, two men stood by them in white apparel; Which also said, Ye men of Galilee, why stand ye gazing up into heaven? this same Jesus which is taken up from you into heaven, shall so come in like manner as ye have seen him go into heaven."

Two angels in the form of men dressed in white explained to the disciples how Jesus will return to that very location (Mount of Olives) in the same way He ascended.

These disciples would receive God's Holy Spirit as Jesus promised. Jesus said He would ascend into heaven to prepare a place for them and He would leave the Holy Spirit with His indwelling presence and power.

John 14:16–17 reads, "And I will pray the Father, and he shall give you another Comforter, that he may abide with you for ever; Even the spirit of truth; whom the world cannot receive, because it seeth him not, neither knoweth him: but ye know him; for he dwelleth with you, and shall be in you."

The disciples were trained by Jesus and were instructed by angels to gain an understanding of what they were experiencing. Once Jesus ascended into heaven the Holy Spirit indwelled the souls of the disciples and taught each of them all things.

Application

Angels are able to appear in human form and may not be immediately recognizable. This was obviously an extremely important event that needed the presence of angels to explain what was going to transpire. The disciples were all experiencing a number of divine moments that could cause a great deal of fear and confusion. These angels were able to explain to the disciples what they were seeing and bring to the disciples a sense of peace and divine glory.

The Rapture

Approximately (unknown)

THE APOSTLE PAUL WAS a man who lived a life that was on the edge. He faced death throughout most of his life, traveled throughout the eastern Mediterranean area and preached to both the Jews and the Gentiles. He was stoned and beaten for his message and was shipwreaked and almost drowned.

However, he continued with God's strength under life threatening conditions, hatred, and illness. He understood and explained that this body we now possess will pass away and we will be given a new spiritual body.

1 Corinthians 15:51–52 reads, "Behold, I show you a mystery; We shall not all sleep, but we shall all be changed, In a moment, in the twinkling of an eye, at the last trump: for the trumpet shall sound, and the dead shall be raised incorruptible, and we shall be changed."

1 Thessalonians 4:16–17 reads, "For the Lord himself shall descend from heaven with a shout, with the voice of the archangel, and the trump of God: and the dead in Christ shall rise first. Then we which are alive and remain shall be caught up together with them in the clouds, to meet the Lord in the air: and so shall we ever be with the Lord."

All believers will be caught up in the air to meet their Lord. Those that have died will be raised from the grave and their souls and spirits will be given a new Christ- like body. The Archangel with God's great power will sound his trump that will raise all believers both dead and alive to meet their Lord and Savior in the sky.

Philippians 3:21 reads, "Who shall change our vile body, that it may be fashioned like unto his glorious body, according to the working whereby he is able even to subdue all things unto himself."

Christians will have glorified bodies that will reflect God's perfections and will no longer be limited by a body that is subject to sin and disease.

Christians will be judged for their accomplishments and God will reward those who have made a difference in people lives. We as Christians have been redeemed at a very high price, the death of God's only Son. Christians remain on this earth for the purpose of bringing others into God's kingdom and proclaiming God's love and grace to all of mankind.

Application

The time when the Rapture will occur is not known by any man. It is believed the first rapture occurred during Jesus' resurrection.

Matthew 27:51–53 reads, "And, behold, the veil of the temple was rent in twain from the top to the bottom: and the earth did quake, and rocks rent; And the graves were opened; and many bodies of the saints which slept arose, And came out of the graves after his resurrection, and went into the holy city, and appeared unto many."

It is believed that the Apostle Matthew included this eye witness account for good reason. A great earthquake did occur that broke open many rocks of the graves of many Old Testament Saints. No doubt, the people of Jerusalem after seeing the saints of the past appear throughout the city came to the realization that Jesus was who he said he was, the Messiah, the Son of God. The veil that separated the Holy of Holies from common man was torn and common man now had direct access to God their Creator. It is believed the Old Testament Saints were raised with Jesus during this time and were given new immortal bodies.

The Rapture will come as a thief in the night when man will least expect it. We need to be prepared and have our priorities in place.

It is believed that many angels will be involved in many different ways.

Tribulation

Approximately (unknown)

IT IS BELIEVED THAT after the Rapture of the church is completed the tribulation will begin.

Matthew 24:3–8 reads, "And as he sat upon the mount of Olives, the disciples came unto him privately, saying, Tell us, when shall these things be? And what shall be the sign of thy coming, and of the end of the world? And Jesus answered and said unto them, Take heed that no man deceive you. For many shall come in my name, saying, I am Christ; and shall deceive many. And ye shall hear of wars and rumors of wars: see that ye be not troubled: for all these things must come to pass, but the end is not yet. For nations shall rise against nations, and kingdom against kingdom: and there shall be famines, and pestilences, and earthquakes, in divers places. All these are the beginning of sorrows."

Angels in heaven will be sounding the trumps of warning that the end is approaching.

Matthew 24:21 reads, "For then shall be great tribulation, such as was not since the beginning of the world to this time, no, nor ever shall be."

Application

The message is that the final period of time for the earth will be marked by many earthquakes, destructive storms, suffering from disease, famine, and many other natural disasters. Many angels will be sounding the alarm that the end is near and people need to worship God and live a life that follows God's commands.

The Second Coming

Approximately (unknown)

AFTER THIS DIFFICULT TIME God will return with His angels and hosts and establish a kingdom for a thousand years on earth.

Revelations 11:15–16 reads, "And the seventh angel sounded; and there were great voices in heaven, saying, The kingdoms of this world are become the kingdoms of our Lord, and of His Christ; and he shall reign for ever and ever. And the four and twenty elders, which sat before God on their seats, fell upon their faces, and worshiped God."

Again, we see that angels are used to bringing about important messages. Angels will be sounding powerful trump blasts to act as a warning to the unbeliever that the final judgment is at hand. Angels will also be used in a number of other different situations.

Revelation 14:6 reads, "And I saw another angel fly in the midst of heaven, having the everlasting gospel to preach unto them that dwell on the earth, and to every nation, and kindred, and tongue, and people."

Angels are used in the final judgment to preach the gospel to unbelievers, to separate unbelievers and believers, to chain Satan and cast him into the abyss.

Revelations 20:1–2 reads, "And I saw an angel come down from heaven, having the key of the bottomless pit and a great chain in his hand. And he laid hold on the dragon, that old serpent, which is the Devil, and Satan, and bound him a thousand years."

Revelations 20:10 reads, "And the devil that deceived them was cast into the lake of fire and brimstone, where the beast and the false prophet are, and shall be tormented day and night for ever and ever."

It is believed that Satan and his many evil follows will be overpowered by God's countless angels and imprisoned for a thousand years and soon after be cast into the lake of fire forever. After the final judgment there will be a new earth and a new heaven where righteousness is achieved and God is ever present. There will be great joy, singing of angels and peace will be the norm.

Application

The second coming of Jesus will be witnessed by all as He appears in the sky with His countless angels. Each person's soul and spiritual life will be laid bare as their lives are reviewed.

Acts 1:11 reads, "Which also said, Ye men of Galilee, why stand ye gazing up into heaven? this same Jesus, which is taken up from you into heaven, shall so come in like manner as ye have seen him go into heaven."

In this situation an angel explains in detail how Jesus will return during His second coming. This message is still repeated today as Christians throughout the world prepare for their Savior and Lord's second coming.

Revelation 1:7 reads, "Behold, he cometh with clouds; and every eye shall see him, and they also which pierced him: and all kindred of the earth shall wail because of him. Even so, Amen."

Countless number of angels will be present with Jesus during His second coming. These angels will fill a number of various important needs. Many will be singing praises and worshiping the Almighty God, the Creator of all and Savior of the world. Many others will be involved in the judgment of mankind and the lives that they lived.

Revelations 20:11–13 reads, "And I saw a great white throne, and him that sat on it, from whose face the earth and the heaven fled away; and thee was found no place for them. And I saw the dead, small and great, stand before God; and the books were opened: and another book was opened, which is the book of life: and the dead were judged out of those things which were written in the books, according to their works. And the sea gave up the dead which were in it; and death and hell delivered up the dead which were in them: and they were judged every man according to their works."

The Bible tells us that the Son of Man will send millions and millions of angels that will gather all the nations, and will separate them one from another as a shepherd separates the sheep from the goats. The Son of Man will also change our human bodies to be like his glorified body.

God's Messengers

There will be two books, one that details the life of those that rejected any belief in God and one that contains the names of all those that accepted eternal life with faith in God. This will be the final judgment.

Revelation

Approximately (7 AD to 100 AD)

IT IS BELIEVED THAT The Apostle John wrote the Book of Revelation while expelled to the island of Patmos. There are many recorded events throughout the Bible where angels filled a number of important functions. They delivered important messages, provided protection, comforted those that were in distress, and worshiped and followed God's commands. Their purpose and function will continue even until the end of creation. God will use angels in the final judgment for all of mankind.

Revelation 5:11–12 reads, "And I beheld, and I heard the voice of many angels round about the throne and the beasts and the elders: and the number of them was ten thousand times ten thousand, and thousands of thousands; Saying with a loud voice, Worthy is the Lamb that was slain to receive power, and riches, and wisdom, and strength, and honor, and glory, and blessing."

The number of angels that will be worshiping and praising God during the final judgment cannot be calculated. Angels will be activity involved in praising both the Father and His Son, Jesus the Christ.

Messenger of Evil

UNFORTUNATELY, THERE ARE MESSENGERS of evil and they have attacked God's love, grace, and peace. Satan was an extremely cunning, beautiful and powerful angel that decided along with his followers to attack God and take control of God's kingdom. They were not successful, but are still rooming the earth looking to devour as many as possible. The truly evil will attack the most vulnerable in society and convert them to the worship of evil.

Today, evil is running out of control due to the fact many people do not believe that God or Satan exist. Many have a vague idea that sin may exist, but have a difficult time defining what actually constitutes sin. Many people live in sinful relationships with other people of like mindedness. They get involved in these relationships and then spend the remainder of their lives trying to convince others that there is nothing wrong with these sinful unions.

Historically, Kings or governments have attacked or punished those that have followed Christianity. In many situations, those that were kings or rulers found the Christian commandments not to be in agreement with their own personal life decisions. Many of these governments or kingdoms were involved in promoting certain gods or mythologies for their own financial benefit. Christianity was seen as a threat to those who were involved in selling services or receiving income from these pagan religious practices. In some cases, kings were highly offended when Christians and their Christian commandments labeled their personal lives as immoral or not in agreement with Jewish law.

Today, well organized groups representing any number of different types of sin have convinced governments to write laws that attack Christian commandments and statutes.

Application

Satan is extremely cunning and was able to convince Eve to disobey God. This sin resulted in the fall of mankind and unleashed disease and death. Since that time, mankind has been condemned to work and struggle to feed himself and his family.

Christians have struggled against governments that have viewed their ministries as a threat to their rule and have passed laws that imposed heavy fines and imprisonment for teaching or meeting to practice Christian beliefs.

1 John 2:16 reads, "For all that is in the world, the lust of the flesh, and the lust of the eyes, and the pride of life, is not of the Father, but is of the world."

Mankind takes great pride in accumulating great wealth and achieving great status. Any person not agreeing with these objectives are discredited and viewed with distain. Mankind takes great pride in their openness and wilingness to accept all people and any value system or religious belief. However, Christians are not accepted due to the fact the Bible does define moral behavior and does not accept all beliefs. The Bible condemns immoral behavior and requires Christians to love God and obey His commandments.

Message of Love for Mankind

ALL OF GOD'S MESSENGERS both angels and humans exhibited great love for God and mankind as they have lived their lives in submission to God's direction. Moses' message for the Israelites was God's love and compassion as He released the Israelites from their bondage and directed them to the Promised Land. God's love was also fulfilled as He molded Moses into a great leader for the Israelites. It was The Apostle James' desire and love for God's people that allowed him to deliver such fiery sermons that those that were in ear shot were moved and recognized that he was speaking of God's truth. The Apostle Peter's love for Jesus was unquestionable. Among the Apostles, Peter was the first in many ways to express his love for Jesus. He was the first to recognize Jesus as the Messiah and the Savior for all mankind. Peter was impetuous and his love for Jesus was obvious as he jumped into the water because he could not wait for the boat to arrive. The Apostle Peter made many mistakes, but Jesus loved him regardless. When Jesus asked Peter three times if he loved him he was devastated. And, when a broken Peter said yes, Jesus said, feed my sheep. The Apostle Peter spent the remainder of his 40 years feeding Jesus' sheep showing his love for both His Lord and neighbor. The Apostle John was a man that Jesus loved for his ability to grasp the importance of biblical truths and teachings. John was a compassionate man and had a heart for those in need.

John 13:1 reads, "Now before the feast of the Passover, when Jesus knew that his hour was come that he should depart out of this world unto the Father, having loved his own which were in the world, he loved them unto the end."

No greater love has ever been seen as when God gave his only Son. No greater humility has ever been experienced as when God's only Son became a servant and teacher to his people. And, finally Jesus' obedience, death, and Resurrection revealed a love that defeated death and opened the door to everlasting life.

God has given to us many messages of love for us to follow. God's messengers all understood the importance of listening and understanding God's word and direction. Moses and Elijah were completely dependent on God for their daily existence. Peter, James, and John were also dependent on God as they preached God's word in a hostile environment where death was a possibility any day. All these men loved their neighbors and were all willing to make the ultimate sacrifice so that they may experience eternal life with their Creator.

We need to remember that the greatest gift is God's love for us and we need to share that gift with our neighbors. There is nothing we could do that would have a greater impact on their lives than to explain the way of salvation. The consequence of this decision is life or death and will last for eternity. Unfortunately, many churches are adrift today and spend more time speaking of social issues and in some cases nothing about salvation. We all need to be prepared to answer the question, have you fed my sheep? What kind of shepherd have you been for God's people? Have you been loving, caring, and thoughtful of others? Have you been willing to be protective of others from the wolves of this world, are you willing to give a helping hand to others, and are you willing to go after the one that is lost?

Message of Spiritual Joy

THE MESSAGE OF SPIRITUAL joy is the fact that the amount of spiritual joy we experience is determined by how we live our lives and share God's love with others. The amount of spiritual joy we experience in our daily lives is controlled by the Holy Spirit within our being. The Holy Spirit communes with us in a way we cannot understand and intercedes for us in our prayers. Unfortunately, the degree and consistency of spiritual joy within our life is affected by our sin. Sin has a lasting and immediate effect on our spirit and soul and will quench the spirit and diminish our spiritual joy.

The degree of spiritual joy will fluctuate and will react to highly spiritual music, preaching, or other messages of God's love and compassion. It is not uncommon for people to be overcome by Spiritual Joy. Another source of spiritual joy is from others in a prayer group or church service.

Hebrews 10:24–25 reads, "And let us consider one another to provoke unto love and to good works: Not forsaking the assembling of ourselves together, as the manner of some is; but exhorting one another: and so much the more, as ye see the day approaching."

The purpose of assembly is to primarily worship and praise the Creator of all things, our great and Almighty God. We love and cherish this time we spend together encouraging each other in resolving life's challenges. We share our concerns and pray for each individual and their unique needs and situation.

As Moses, we need to consider all of God's blessings and realize that He is the one and only God and the Creator of all. Moses had great spiritual joy when he saw what God had done for the Israelites.

Exodus 15:1–5 reads, "Then sang Moses and the children of Israel this song unto the Lord, and spake, saying, I will sing unto the Lord, for he hath triumphed gloriously: the horse and his rider hath he thrown into the sea. The Lord is my strength and song, and he become my salvation: he is my

God, and I will prepare him a habitation; my father's God, and I will exalt him. The Lord is man of war: the Lord is his name. Pharaoh's chariots and his host hath he cast into the sea: his chosen captains also are drowned in the Red Sea. The depths have covered them: they sank into the bottom as a stone."

Moses and the Israelites sang a song of great joy and praise knowing that the hand of the Lord had protected them from Pharaoh's army and certain death and slavery. We know that the Creator of the universe with His mighty powers and with greatness of majesty is our personal Lord and Savior and that He has placed His hand of protection over us each day. He is with us daily and directs us away from the Pharaoh's of this world. Our hearts are full of spiritual joy as we sing and praise our Lord and Savior. We fall on our faces as we ask for redemption from our pride of life and our sin nature.

Elijah was a man who wrestled with his expectations for how events should unfold. It wasn't until he realized that God was in control regardless of his own expectations that he was able to fully understand and appreciate the sweet comfort of spiritual joy. God is in control as to how events unfold in our daily lives. We are responsible for being obedient to God's word, to submit our requests in prayer, and to be faithful in all things. We rest in Him putting all of our trust in Him knowing He loves us and is preparing our way.

2 Corinthians 5:5–7 reads, "Now he that hath wrought us for the self-same thing is God, who also hath given unto us the earnest of the spirit. Therefore we are always confident, knowing that, whilst we are at home in the body, we are absent from the Lord. For we walk by faith, not by sight."

Our souls long to be with our Creator and Lord. And, our souls jump with joy as we experience spiritual joy when we hear His words in song, in testimony, and in reading. Our spiritual joy increases as we learn to view our life in its proper perspective. We need to focus on the final goal and prepare ourselves for an eternal life with our Lord and Savior.

Peter realized that spiritual joy can be realized when fear has been conquered through faith.

1 Peter 1:6 reads, "Wherein ye greatly rejoice, though now for a season, if need be, ye are in heaviness through manifold temptations."

When we succeed against temptations we grow in faith and we experience spiritual joy. Faith grows stronger when tested with trials and temptations and we finally realize we can always put our faith in the Lord to carry us through any situation.

God changed Peter from a selfish, self-centered man with many frailties into a spirit-filled vessel capable of healing those with infirmities. Peter's spiritual joy was experienced with trials and struggles knowing God was pruning away his sinful nature.

1 Peter 4:13 reads, "But rejoice, inasmuch as ye are partakers of Christ's sufferings; that, when his glory shall be revealed, ye may be glad also with exceeding joy."

1 Peter 1:7 reads, "That the trial of your faith, being much more precious than of gold that perisheth, though it be tried with fire, might be found unto praise and honor and glory at the appearing of Jesus Christ."

We run a race with countless numbers of angels in heaven cheering us on as we strengthen our endurance and conquer each new challenge. We are waiting to hear the words, "well done my good and faithful servant."

Matthew 25:21 reads, "His Lord said unto him, Well done, thou good and faithful servant: thou hast been faithful over a few things, I will make thee ruler over many things: enter thou into the joy of thy Lord."

The Apostle James' (Son of Thunder) spiritual joy was amazing. He was the oldest Apostle and one of the most spiritually mature with a gift for speaking. His heart was fixed on delivering the message of salvation to all who would listen and his spiritual joy was increased as new believers made decisions to follow the teaching of Jesus the Messiah.

Philippians 4:4 reads, "Rejoice in the Lord always: and again I say, Rejoice."

The Apostle James rejoiced in the Lord always regardless of the circumstance. God is in control of all things and we are simply responsible for being obedient to His word, loving our neighbor, and praising and thanking Him for all blessings.

The Apostle James was part of the inner circle of Apostles and was under Jesus' teaching for three years, was present during the raising of Jairus' daughter, was in the Garden of Gethsemane with Jesus, and was present to see Jesus after the Resurrection. The Apostle James spoke with authority, with complete confidence, and with the power of the Holy Spirit. The Apostle James was filled by the Holy Spirit and experienced great spiritual joy.

Acts 12:1–3 reads, "Now about that time Herod the king stretched forth his hands to vex certain of the church. And he killed James the brother of John with the sword. And because he saw it pleased the Jews, he proceeded further to take Peter also. (Then were the days of unleavened bread.)"

The Apostle James joy was not tied to this earth and its possessions, prestige, success, or reputation. He was a vessel filled with the Holy Spirit. The spiritual joy James experienced came from the knowledge that the souls that were saved would experience eternity with their Lord and Savior. The rejoicing in heaven is beyond our comprehension.

The Apostle John (the beloved disciple) was an Apostle whose life was centered on his love for His Lord and Savior and his love for his neighbor.

1 John 1:4 reads, "And these things write we unto you, that your joy may be full."

John was sharing his personal experience of knowing his Lord and Savior and the joy that it brought him each day. John's joy was due to the fact his entire life was centered on God and his relationship with God. Consequently, his joy was not affected by circumstances or by the increase or decrease of possessions, prestige, reputation, or any other earthly pleasure. His joy was directly related to having the Holy Spirit fill him each day with joy as he praised and thanked God for his many blessings and continued to minister to God's people and the church.

Today the world and man are driven by expectations and how to achieve the next goal of wealth, possession, or position. The Apostle John and the other Apostles achieved spiritual joy by furthering the gospel and building the church. Our joy is also achieved by furthering the gospel and seeing how God's kingdom is expanded with each new soul.

Luke 15: 4–7 reads, "What man of you, having a hundred sheep, if he lose one of them, doth not leave the ninety and nine in the in wilderness, and go after that which is lost, until he find it? And when he hath found it, he layeth it on his shoulders, rejoicing. And when he cometh home, he calleth together his friends and neighbors, saying unto them, rejoice with me; for I have found my sheep which was lost. I say unto you, that likewise joy shall be in heaven over one sinner that repenteth, more than over ninety and nine just persons, which need no repentance."

Man is God's creation and is of more value then we can comprehend. The purpose of the church is to care for and nourish the souls that attend and to search for those that are lost. Our churches should be focused on the conversion of those that have not made the decision to follow Jesus' teachings. Our church services should be filled with testimonies of those that have surrendered their life to Christ and have made a change in their life. The members of the church need to be experiencing spiritual joy along with those in heaven as testimonies are told of the lives that have been changed. We were created for the purpose of praising God for His unbelievable gifts and blessings.

Message of God's Gift of His Son

GOD'S MESSAGE TO THE believer is that He is watching over them, protecting them, and providing them a peace that they cannot explain.

Philippians 4:6–7 reads, "Be careful for nothing; but in everything by prayer and supplication with thanksgiving let your requests be made known unto God. And the peace of God, which passeth all understanding, shall keep your hearts and minds through Christ Jesus."

God is in control and there is no reason to worry. It is the believer's responsibility to bring all of his concerns to God in prayer. And, to bring all of his prayers of concerns with thanksgiving for the blessings he has received. It is important that we realize all that we are or ever will be is from God's love, mercy, and grace.

Moses knew of God's peace and how God is in control and how He provides new paths as old ones are closed.

Exodus 14:13–14 reads, "And Moses said unto the people, Fear ye not, stand still, and see the salvation of the Lord, which he will show to you today: for the Egyptians whom ye have seen today, ye shall see them again no more for ever. The Lord shall fight for you, and ye shall hold your peace."

We are to stand still and be quiet and wait for the Lord to provide direction. Our minds and thoughts should be focused on all of God's blessings, how He has comforted us, and how He has been faithful in so many ways and for so many years. From the beginning of time God has been there to love us and care for us.

Exodus 33:11 reads, "And the lord spake unto Moses face to face, as a man speaketh unto a friend. And he turned again into the camp: but his servant Joshua, the son of Nun, a young man, departed not out of the tabernacle."

Exodus 33:14 reads, "And he said, My presence shall go with thee, and I will give thee rest."

God's Messengers

God spoke to Moses as a friend speaks to a friend and God promised that He would be with Moses and give him rest. Moses found grace and peace with God and would call him by name. God's divine presence and mighty majesty carried Moses to unfold great miracles to be accomplished for the Israelites.

Elijah was also given peace and comfort from God.

1 Kings 19:7 reads, "And the angel of the lord came again the second time, and touched him, and said, Arise and eat; because the journey is too great for thee."

God provided Elijah with nourishment and rest that would sustain him for a long and difficult journey through the desert. God was aware of Elijah's physical condition; the dangers he faced, and was ensuring that Elijah would be successful in unfolding God's plan and miracles.

God is continually providing protection and nourishment for those that follow His direction. We need to take every opportunity to thank God for His nourishment, protection, and unwavering faithfulness.

2 Kings 2:11 reads, "And it came to pass, as they still went on, and talked, that, behold, there appeared a chariot of fire, and horses of fire, and parted them both asunder; and Elijah went up by a whirlwind into heaven."

God was pleased with Elijah and collected him from this earth with a mighty display of His power. Elijah did not experience death and he was taken directly into God's presence. No army, no force can compare with God's power and might. Elijah was placed under great pressure and feared for not being obedient to God's will. God responded by placing Elijah in heaven where he experienced complete peace and joy.

We need to remember that we may experience difficult times, but our journey ends in complete peace with our Creator and Lord for eternity.

The Apostle Peter continually reminded the church that peace and grace would increase as the knowledge of Jesus Christ increased.

2 Peter 1:1–2 reads, "Simon Peter, a servant and an apostle of Jesus Christ, to them that have obtained like precious faith with us through the righteousness of God and our Savior Jesus Christ. Grace and peace be multiplied unto you through the knowledge of God, and of Jesus our Lord."

We are to be fully engaged in taking advantage of our personal relationship with our Creator to experience the full impact of His peace and grace in our daily life. His peace and grace gives us the knowledge to break free from the world and all of it's evil desires and lusts. The world and it's obsession with wealth is extremely dangerous and will cause men to kill, steal, and destroy entire families. In some ways, the desire for wealth is like an addictive drug that will take control of every decision. This addiction will dictate standards for ethics, morals, and how men view his neighbor.

Romans 5:1–2 reads, "Therefore being justified by faith, we have peace with God through our Lord Jesus Christ. By whom also we have access by faith into this grace wherein we stand, and rejoice in hope of the glory of God."

We have been justified by our faith in the Lord Jesus Christ. Jesus Christ paid the price for us to enjoy the great peace that is available to all that have faith. As we travel through this journey of life we need to rejoice in all of God's blessings and rest in the peace that is beyond our understanding.

1 Peter 5:6–7 reads, "Humble yourselves therefore under the mighty hand of God, that he may exalt you in due time. Casting all your cares upon him; for he careth for you."

Our life has been turned over to God and His will. We wait and act in complete humility and prayer looking and listening for His direction and will for our life. We need to remember all those who have been martyred, those that have sacrificed everything, and the ultimate gift of God's only Son. We need to approach our Savior and Lord on our knees in complete humility.

The Holy Spirit is part of the Trinity and at the same time a separate entity within the same Deity. He is also called the great Comforter because of the Holy Spirit's ability to provide peace to people when they are under severe conflict, pain, and suffering. The peace that is provided by the Holy Spirit is a very unique peace that only the Holy Spirit is able to provide.

John 14:26–27 reads, "But the Comforter, which is the Holy Ghost, whom the Father will send in my name, he shall teach you all things, and bring all things to your remembrance, whatsoever I have said unto you. Peace I leave with you, my peace I give unto you: not as the world giveth, give I unto you. Let not your heart be troubled, neither let it be afraid."

The believer receives the glorious gift of the Holy Spirit when a decision is made and a confession of faith is declared. This is the same Holy Spirit that Peter received at Pentecost that allowed him to preach with such conviction that over 3,000 were baptized and converted to following Jesus' teachings. Most believers do not realize the power of the Holy Spirit within their life. The believer that is obedient to God's commands, has placed their full faith in our loving God, is thankful for all of God's blessings, will experience the peace of the Holy Spirit. The Holy Spirit is able to provide many blessings, such as confidence, the appropriate words in a difficult situation, love, compassion, and awareness of others situations, open opportunities that would not otherwise be available, and bringing people into your life for support and perspective. These are just a few of the blessings associated with living a life that allows the Holy Spirit to take up residence within your life and gives you God's peace.

Colossians 1:20 reads, "And, having made peace through the blood of his cross, by him to reconcile all things unto himself: by him, I say, whether they be things in earth, or things in heaven."

God's peace that was given to sinful man was only possible because of Jesus' sacrifice and His blood that was shed on the cross. The believer receives this peace daily because of the Holy Spirit's continual intercession for us as we struggle with daily challenges due to our weaknesses and temptations. This peace is God's peace and cannot be explained by man.

Psalm 139: 1–6 reads, "O Lord thou hast searched me, and know me. Thou knowest my downsitting, and mine upraising; thou understandest my thoughts afar off. Thou compassest my path and my lying down, and art acquainted with all my ways. For there is not a word in my tongue, but, lo, O Lord, thou knows it altogether. Thou hast beset me behind and before, and laid thine hand upon me. Such knowledge is too wonderful for me; it is high, I cannot attain unto it."

As believers we place our complete trust in Jesus, we place Him at the center of our life, and wait patiently under His peace for His direction. Only God knows the true way for our life and we need to surrender to His direction. His path for our lives has been prepared and we need walk under his protection.

The Apostle John was a man of Jesus' love and peace.

John 20:19–22 reads, "Then the same day at evening, being the first day of the week, when the doors were shut where the disciples were assembled for fear of the Jews, came Jesus and stood in the midst, and saith unto them, Peace be unto you. And when he had so said, he showed unto them his hands and his side. Then were the disciples glad, when they saw the Lord. Then said Jesus to them again, Peace be unto you: as my Father hath sent me, even so send I you. And when he had said this, he breathed on them, and saith unto them, Receive ye the Holy Ghost."

The Apostle John and others were meeting behind locked doors in fear not knowing if they would be the next to be arrested and possibly crucified. The miraculous appearance of Jesus in this room gave the disciples the peace that passes all understanding. This type of peace erased all doubt, established confidence, and fulfilled their faith. They were in fact vessels that were now prepared to receive the Holy Spirit. At this point, the Holy Spirit was able to transform each of the disciples and work with them individually to carry out God's plan. At some time later, all believers were baptized by the Holy Spirit at Pentecost and were sent out speaking many different languages.

The Apostle John understood the meaning of peace and spoke of peace to the churches he ministered.

John 16:33 reads, "These things I have spoken unto you, that in me ye might have peace. In the world ye shall have tribulation: but be of good cheer; I have overcome the world."

Believers have made a decision to follow Jesus Christ and His teachings and are therefore walking with the Holy Spirit in God's plan. However, believers are still in this world and pressured by Satan and his demons. The Apostle John in this verse was reminding these believers to be at peace in knowing God is in control and he has beaten evil at every step. As believers we are to rest in God's grace knowing our sins were forgiven by the sacrifice of God's only Son.

As natural men we have many frailties and a fallen nature that invades our daily life with many distractions that are destructive to living a Christ centered life.

John 14: 27 reads, "Peace I leave with you, my peace I give unto you: not as the world giveth, give I unto you. Let not your heart be troubled, neither let it be afraid."

We are bombarded each day by a world that has a set of morals and ethics that are based on pleasure, pride of life, and greed. As our society continues to crumble with no moral or ethical guide, our leadership does not provide any type of direction for reversing a path to civil anarchy. The lack of respect for another person, the sense of entitlement, and the act of killing another person for no reason is the result of a society without values or morals.

The peace that a believer receives is not from the world or from anything that is related to the world. Peace from God is not related to wealth, pleasure, or any other aspect of worldly living. A believer's peace comes from knowing that they are living in God's will, they have eternal security, God will supply for their needs, and God will direct them as to which path to follow.

A natural man (e.g., carnal man, fallen man) is a man that is completely dependent on physical things and unable to receive and preserve spiritual blessings from the Holy Spirit. A natural man is completely possessed by physical desires, senses of pleasures, taste, touch, emotions, pride of life, and ego. He is controlled by his eyes and heart as he lusts for evil, for status, and wealth.

1 Corinthians 2:14 reads, "But the natural man received not the things of the spirit of God: for they are foolishness unto him: neither can he know them, because they are spiritually discerned."

A natural man takes on many of the characteristics of Satan and his demons as he goes through life self absorbed and dispensing evil to those that get in his way. The soul and spirit of the natural man escapes into a deep hibernation and can only be awaken by the Holy Spirit.

The spiritual man knows the voice of the Lord and is able to experience peace knowing he is in God's will.

John 10:3–5 reads, "To him the porter openeth; and the sheep hear his voice: and he calleth his own sheep by name, and leadeth them out. And when he putteth forth his own sheep, he goeth before them, and the sheep follow him: for they know his voice. And a stranger will they not follow, but will fee from him: for they know not the voice of strangers."

God calls each individual by name and leads them through their life. God's leading is obvious when people look back over their life and see how God has open doors, changed events, and used others to lead or change their attitudes.

To grow in our faith we need to realize that the goals and values of the world are not God's goals and values. His direction for our life may not be what we want for our life. And, to hear God's voice requires us to change how we think and to train our minds to close out the noise of the world and to allow His Spirit to take control of our thoughts. God's speaks to each of us throughout each day.

John 4:24 reads, "God is a Spirit: and they that worship him must worship him in spirit and in truth."

The Holy Spirit communes with the spiritual man in ways that are not understood by the natural man. The Holy Spirit acts as a conduit between man and God as He creates ideas and impressions within a spiritual man's life. These thoughts and impressions are given frequently throughout each day to man for developing ideas and impressions. The gift of the Holy Spirit to a spiritual man brings great peace, joy, and allows him to rejoice in the knowledge he is in God's will. A spiritual man's life has purpose and that purpose is following God's direction.

The natural man worships his possessions and all other things and has stopped his soul and spirit from functioning. Sin and Satan has blinded the natural man and caused him to consider worshiping God as foolishness.

1 Kings 19:12 reads, "And after the earthquake a fire, but the Lord was not in the fire: and after the fire a still small voice."

Elijah, a spiritual man, was able to hear this still small voice. Elijah's heart and mind knew God's voice and was able to recognize that it was God speaking to him. It is when we are silent and separated from the world our spirit begins to hear and recognize God's thoughts and impressions. The thoughts we receive from our spirit are not like most thoughts. They are like whispers that are easily forgotten in a manner of minutes. In most cases they need to be written down before they are lost.

Proverbs 24:3-4 reads, "Through wisdom is a house builded; and by understanding it, is established. And by knowledge shall the chambers be filled with all precious and pleasant riches."

Every person has a spirit and soul; however few people understand it or know how to care for it. The natural man has a mind that is completely consumed by thoughts and ideas based on the world's values and ethics. In most cases any thought of a spiritual nature is immediately discarded. The natural man's mind is at war with the spiritual and will drown out any spiritual thought or distract the mind with other thoughts. Controlling your thoughts or selecting thoughts is difficult and requires God's strength and direction.

Isaiah 11:2 reads, "And the spirit of the Lord shall rest upon him, the spirit of wisdom and understanding, the spirit of counsel and might, the spirit of knowledge and the fear of the Lord."

Most people need to set aside some time each day to be at peace with God's word and allow the Holy Spirit to commune with our spirit. In prayer we praise His name, thank Him for the gift of His Son and His many daily blessings, ask for forgiveness for our many sins, and submit our requests and concerns. We need to be at rest to allow our spirit and mind to focus on what is really a priority.

Message of Longsuffering

God's plan for mankind and how He unfolds His plan is only known to God. Generally, we are able to see God's plans as we look back over many years. It's only when we come to the realization and understanding that God is in control and we are able to turn over all of our concerns over to God and experience God's peace.

We are all at times placed in situations where we need to be patient and endure difficulties. As we go through these circumstances we begin to develop strength and are better able to endure persecution. The growing in faith and communing with the Holy Spirit is directly related to developing patience and endurance in difficult situations. It is extremely important that we allow the Holy Spirit to take control in difficult situations. The Holy Spirit is able to carry us through difficult times and to provide a resting place for our emotions and mind. Some of us go through a lifetime of difficult situations and have survived simply by turning over all fear, hate, and sin in prayer to God.

Ephesians 3:10–15, "To the intent that now unto the principalities and powers in heavenly places might be know by the church the manifold wisdom of God. According to the eternal purpose which be purposed in Christ Jesus our Lord: In whom we have boldness and access with confidence by the faith of him. Wherefore I desire that ye faint not at my tribulations for you, which is your glory. For this cause I bow my knees unto the Father of our Lord Jesus Christ. Of whom the whole family in heaven and earth is named."

We are a member of a family of believers that number in the millions that are both in heaven and on earth. All of these members have derived their faith from God our Creator and He now counts each one of us as His own.

Message of Longsuffering

The Jewish people suffered greatly for hundreds of years as slaves under the barbaric rule of the Egyptians until God called Moses to lead them to the Promised Land. Even then the Jewish people suffered as they wandered the desert for 40 years because of lack of faith and the sin of building pagan gods. God strengthened Moses and gave Moses the endurance to experience the longsuffering of leading over 600,000 people through the desert.

Exodus 34:5-6 reads, "And the Lord descended in the cloud, and stood with him there, and proclaimed the name of the Lord. And the Lord passed by before him, and proclaimed, The Lord, The Lord God, merciful and gracious, long-suffering, and abundant in goodness and truth."

God is merciful and patient with us as we struggle with sin in a world that is lost in pride of life, distorted values, and the refusal to recognize all of God's blessings.

Psalm 103:7-14 reads, "He made known his ways unto Moses, his acts unto the children of Israel. The Lord is merciful and gracious, slow to anger, and plenteous in mercy. He will not always chide: neither will he keep his anger forever. He hath not dealt with us after our sins, nor rewarded us according to our iniquities. For as the heavens is high above the earth, so great is his mercy toward them that fear him. As far as the east is from the west, so far hath he removed our transgressions from us. Like as a father pitieth his children, so the Lord pitieth them that fear him. For he knoweth our frame; he remembereth that we are dust."

God was slow to anger with both Moses and the Israelites; he is merciful, patient, and gives us time to repent of our sins. We need to approach our Lord and Savior with a contrite heart, with weeping, asking for forgiveness and asking for His mercy.

Elijah was a man who suffered greatly under the rule of King Ahab and Jezebel for not worshiping the pagan god Baal. King Ahab and Jezebel were extremely wicked rulers that were under the influence of Satan that forced all people to worship Baal and other pagan gods. This worship included many temple prostitutes and many other unspeakable acts of human degradation.

Mark 7:21-23 reads, "For from within, out of the heart of men, proceed evil thoughts, adulteries, fornication, murders. Thefts, covetousness, wickedness, deceit, lasciviousness, an evil eye, blasphemy, pride, foolishness: All these evil things come from within, and defile the man."

The natural man is full of evil and it is apparent in the words he uses, the thoughts he entertains, and the actions he takes. However, those that are believers are given the Holy Spirit that leads and instructs man in ways that are pleasing to God. We live in a world that is lost in sin and suffering and we experience that suffering as Christ experienced that suffering. However, we need to remember that we are only here for a short time and the suffering we encounter is insignificant compared to the glory that we will experience as God pores out His never ending love upon us. All of creation will bear the pain of a new birth when Christ returns to claim his own.

Revelation 21:1–4, reads, "And I saw a new heaven and a new earth, for the first heaven and the first earth were passed away: and there was no more sea. And I John saw the holy city, new Jerusalem, coming down from God out of heaven, prepared as a bride adorned for her husband. And I heard a great voice out of heaven saying, Behold, the tabernacle of God is with men, and he will dwell with them, and they shall be his people, and God himself shall be with them, and be their God. And God shall wipe away all tears from their eyes; and there shall be no more death, neither sorrow, nor crying, neither shall there be any more pain: for the former things are passed away."

Elijah was completely dependent on God for his entire life. He obeyed God when he approached King Ahab and prophesied a drought that would last for three years. We need to be obedient to God's direction and wait patiently for the next door to be opened. We all go through difficult times and we all are subject to tests. However, the only way to grow in faith and to be redeemed out of this world is to go through suffering and tests. We can all rest in the knowledge that God's love will only allow those sufferings and trials in our life that are for our benefit.

Troubling events and problems affect all of mankind in some way. For some, these events have a dramatic impact on their life, whereas others these same events have different or little impact. The believer through their faith has the power and grace of the Holy Spirit in their life and can at any time request His peace in prayer. God deals with each individual in ways that addresses his or her faith.

God took Elijah out of complete obscurity and used him to turn thousands of people from pagan worship to the worship of the one and true God. As Moses, Elijah experienced the power and grace of God Our Father. He also experienced the long-suffering as Jesus Christ did in being obedient to God and following His direction.

Romans 11:33 reads, "O the depth of the riches both of the wisdom and knowledge of god! how unsearchable are his judgments, and his ways past finding out."

God's paths and ways are never ending and are available for all believers to search and experience His blessings.

When we suffer as believers we are being identified with the suffering of Jesus on the cross. Suffering provides a way for us to prove our faith in our Lord and Savior.

Peter had firsthand knowledge of the suffering of Jesus as He hung on the cross to be a sacrifice for all the sins of mankind.

1 Peter 1:22–25 reads, "Seeing ye have purified your soul in obeying the truth through the Spirit unto unfeigned love of the brethren, see that ye love one another with a pure heart fervently. Being born again, not of corruptible seed, but of incorruptible, by the word of God, which liveth and abideth for ever. For all flesh is as grass, and all the glory of man as the flowers of grass. The grass withereth, and the flowers thereof falleth away: But the word of the Lord endureth for ever. And this is the word which by the gospel is preached unto you."

As we live through suffering our focus as believers is to purify our souls as we obey God's commands to love the Lord with all our heart and to love your neighbor as our self. We long for the word of God because it provides nourishment for our souls and allows us access to His glory.

1 Peter 4:12–14 reads, "Beloved think it not strange concerning the fiery trial which is to try you, as though some strange thing happen unto you. But rejoice inasmuch as ye are partakers of Christ's suffering; that, when his glory shall be revealed, ye may be glad also with exceeding joy. If ye be reproached for the name of Christ, happy are ye; for the spirit of glory and of God resteth upon you: on their part he is evil spoken of, but on your part he is glorified."

If you suffer because you are a believer you will be blessed and identified with the glory of God. Suffering for Christ is a reason for rejoicing because it identifies the believer with Christ. Sharing the suffering of Christ allows a believer to take part in His glory, to commune in joy with the Holy Spirit, and is a privilege.

The Apostle Peter considered the long-suffering of the believer as the process one goes through to refine their faith. A believer continues to deal with sin on a daily basis and may fail and may be disciplined.

1 Peter 4:19 reads, "Wherefore let them that suffer according to the will of God commit the keeping of their souls to him in well doing, as unto a faithful Creator."

As believers we continue to live a holy life by entrusting our souls to our Creator who judges justly and indentifies himself with the faithful. Just as Christ entrusted Himself to the Father, so do we need to entrust our souls to our Lord and Savior.

1 Peter 3:12 reads, "For the eyes of the Lord are over the righteous, and his ears are open unto their prayers: But the face of the Lord is against them that do evil."

The Apostle Peter reminded his followers that obedience to God's word was the best defense against unjust punishment and persecution. Believers are able to overcome fear by being sanctified in Gods' word.

Any person that witnessed the Crucifixion and Resurrection of Jesus would know the truth that Jesus was God and would hold fast to their faith regardless of the danger or risk of death.

1 Corinthians 13:4–5 reads, "Charity suffereth long, and is kind; charity envieth not; charity vaunteth not itself, is not puffed up. Doth not behave itself unseemly, seeketh not her own, is not easily provoked, thinketh no evil;"

A believer's long-suffering involves being patient and not to strike back. Long-suffering also involves showing love, kindness, and goodness. Our Lord is slow to anger and great in mercy. Our faith is built upon long-suffering, patience, and trusting God to provide us with our needs. There are many who can testify of living a life where they can detail where God has created opportunities where there was no hope.

Isaiah 40:31 reads, "But they that wait upon the Lord shall renew their strength; they shall mount up with wings as eagles; they shall run, and not be weary; and they shall walk, and not faint."

We as believers need to be patient and long-suffering as we place our trust in God's leading. We are completely dependent on the Holy Spirit for wisdom and understanding as we present our requests in prayer and thanksgiving. We wait on God for He knows the best time for when we will be ready and when events are to fall into place.

Ephesians 4:1–3 reads, "I therefore, the prisoner of the Lord, beseech you that ye walk worthy of the vocation wherewith ye are called. With all lowliness and meekness, with long-sufffering, forbearing one another in love; Endeavoring to keep the unity of the spirit in the bond of peace."

Message of Longsuffering

A believer's daily walk is in complete humility and in complete obedience to God. A Christian that is fully controlled by God is angry only at the right time and only for the right reason. Jesus became angry when the temple was being used by thieves to steal from the poor.

The Apostle John was the younger brother of James and a son of Zebedee and Salome. The Apostle John had a home in Jerusalem and it is believed that is where Mary the mother Jesus lived after the Crucifixion. The Apostle John was persecuted and beaten as the other Apostles throughout his life.

Revelations 1: 9–11 reads, "I John, who also am your brother, and companion in tribulation, and in the kingdom and patience of Jesus Christ, was in the isle that is called Patmos, for the word of God, and for the testimony of Jesus Christ. I was in the Spirit on the Lord's day, and heard behind the me a great voice, as of a trumpet. Saying, I am Alpha and Omega, the first and the last: and, What thou seest, write in a book, and send it unto the seven churches which are in Asia; unto Ephesus, and unto Smyrna, and unto Pergamos, and unto Thyatira, and unto Sardis, and unto Philadelphia, and unto Laodicea."

The Apostle John moved to Ephesus and later in his ministry he was imprisoned and sent to the island of Patmos for preaching the word of God and testifying as a witness to Jesus' Crucifixion and Resurrection. On Patmos, the Apostle John was living and working in a mining community. In spite of being imprisoned and subject to hard labor the Apostle John maintained his close relationship with his Lord and Savior. John was under the protection and strength of God that allowed him to experience the long-suffering and the patience to place all his trust in God.

We all go through difficult times of long-suffering where we need to develop patience and realize we need to place all of trust in our Lord and Savior. God is involved in virtually every aspect of our life. God is omniscient, omnipotent, and omnipresent. God knows all things, he knows our thoughts and our words before we speak. God has unlimited power, He created the heaven and earth. God is always present; he is present in our thoughts. Few people have a good understanding of our personal relationship with our Lord and Savior. Their prayers are generally limited and are restricted to only a few times during the day.

Hebrews 13:5 reads, "Let your conversion be without covetousness; and be content with such things as ye have for he hath said, I will never leave thee, nor forsake thee."

God is with us throughout each day and wants a personal relationship with Him as we encounter challenges and distractions. Our first response to all challenges is to first turn them over to God for His direction and power. God is our Lord and Savior, our friend and comforter and He will answer our prayers in His time in a way that is best for us. The Holy Spirit will comfort our spirits and provide thoughts and ideas as to how to resolve problems.

Colossians 3:23 reads, "And whatsoever ye do, do it hearty, as to the Lord, and not unto men."

As believers we work using all of our skills and talents to provide the best possible service or product. God has blessed us with work that we may glorify Him so that we may be a good testimony to others. A worker that follows directions, shows genuine concern, and is able to exceed expectations is valued by all.

Message of Kindness

As believers it is critical that we follow God's direction and allow his love, mercy and kindness to flow through us to those who are waiting for God's intervention. As believers our lives are all woven together as a fine tapestry working as one to form the master piece of God's creation.

The natural or fallen man's morals or ethics are primarily based on pleasure or what feels good and kindness is not a consideration. If it feels good it must be right. There is no reference to the Bible or church teachings. Consequently, greed, pride, and pleasure take control of most of the attitudes, emotions, and decisions made by the natural man.

God's word and commands in many cases are the complete opposite of what the world considers to be appropriate. One of the most repeated commands in the Bible is to love your neighbor. This one command in many cases is probably one of the most forgotten or ignored commands by the world. As believers we are representatives of God's message that He loved all people and gave His only Son that all who would believe would have eternal life. A believer has access to God's power, mercy and grace through prayer. Praying for a neighbor is in most cases the greatest gift or the most effective way of making a difference in a neighbor's life.

1 Samuel 16:7 reads, "But the Lord said unto Samuel, Look not on his countenance, or on height of his stature; because I have refused him: for the Lord seeth not as man seeth; for man looketh on the outward appearance, but the Lord looketh on the heart."

The world values a man by the number of his possessions, wealth, and his position within society. However, God through Samuel selected David to be the next King of Israel because of his heart. David was the youngest son of the family and worked as a shepherd for the family's sheep. But more importantly, God knew David's heart and knew He could mold David into a King that would further His kingdom. God values man by the condition of his heart and his kindness, mercy, and love that he shows to his neighbor.

Titus 3:4–5 reads, "But after that the kindness and love of God our Savior toward man appeared. Not by works of righteousness which we have done, but according to his mercy he saved us, by the washing of regenerataion, and renewing of the Holy Ghost."

Kindness is a gift from God to man for the purpose of allowing man to share this kindness with his neighbor. A believer is blessed beyond measure by the Holy Spirit who enters a man's life when he opens his heart and places his trust and faith in his Savior.

The natural or fallen man is enslaved to pleasure, to self, and the lust of the flesh. God knew of the hurt, suffering and lack of hope in a world where man's heart was not filled with kindness for his fellow man. It was only God's mercy and kindness that broke Satan's shackles of sin, hatred of fellow man, and lust of the flesh. The Holy Spirit changes a man's heart to be obedient to God's word and to give hope where there is no hope, to change an attitude of resignation to an attitude of achievement, and to change hate to love for his neighbor.

The emotional and impetuous Peter was an Apostle who had great love for his Lord and Savior.

2 Peter 1:1–7 reads, "Simon Peter, a servant and an apostle of Jesus Christ, to them that have obtained like precious faith with us through the righteousness of God and our Savior Jesus Christ. Grace and peace be multiplied unto you through the knowledge of God, and of Jesus our Lord. According as his divine power hath given unto us all things that pertain unto life and godliness, through the knowledge of him that hath called us to glory and virtue. Whereby are given unto us exceeding great and precious promises: that by these ye might be partakers of the divine nature, having escaped the corruption that is in the world through lust. And beside this, giving all diligence, add to your faith virtue, and to virtue knowledge. And to knowledge temperance; and to temperance patience; and to patience godliness; And to godliness brotherly kindness; and to brotherly kindness charity."

The Apostle Peter understood the lifelong struggle of spiritual maturity that begins with faith that is based on the righteousness of God and our Savior Jesus the Christ. Faith opens the door to peace and spiritual knowledge. Spiritual knowledge allows for the understanding of God's truths with patience, self control, and without the world's corruption.

Message of Kindness

The Apostle Peter was also aware of those who were suffering and followed Jesus' example in showing mercy and kindness to those who were in need.

Acts 9:32–35 reads, "And it came to pass, as Peter passed throughout all quarters, he came down also to the saints which dwelt at Lydda. And there he found a certain man named Aeneas, which had kept his bed eight years, and was sick of the palsy. And Peter said unto him, Anneas, Jesus Christ maketh thee whole: arise, and make thy bed. And he arose immediately. And all that dwelt at Lydda and Saron saw him, and turned to the Lord."

Peter called upon the name of Jesus and allowed the power of His spirit to flow through him to heal Aeneas of the palsy. This act of kindness and mercy had a profound effect on Lydda and Saron and the entire community returned to worshiping the one and true God.

The Apostle also traveled to Joppa where he healed a woman named Tabitha (Dorcas).

Acts 9: 40–43 reads, "But Peter put them all forth, and kneeled down, and prayed; and turning him to the body said, Tabitha, arise. And she opened her eyes, and when she saw Peter, she sat up."

Tabitha (Dorcas) was a woman full of good works and a believer. Peter's heart was touched by the generosity of this woman and those that testified of her many works of kindness. God saw that this woman had provided great service to the church. Peter prayed that she might continue so that others may receive the blessings of her service.

1 Peter 1:22 reads, "Seeing ye have purified your soul in obeying the truth through the Spirit unto unfeigned love of the brethren, see that ye love one another with a pure heart fervently."

The message is clear. If you want to know God it is essential that you love your neighbors and show them kindness. Jesus also stated that others would be able to identify you as a believer because of your kindness to your neighbor. This one principle is extremely important for a believer to grow and develop a relationship with their Lord and Savior. Other issues that will prevent or block communion with the Holy Spirit are sinfulness, greed, selfishness, and the lack of compassion for the poor and those in need.

Acts 5:15–16 reads, "Insomuch that they brought forth the sick into the streets, and laid them on beds and couches, that at the least the shadow of Peter passing by might overshadow some of them. There came also a multitude out of the cities round about unto Jerusalem, bringing sick folks, and them which were vexed with unclean spirits: and they were healed every one."

Mark 16:15–18 reads, "And he said unto them, Go ye into the world, and preach the gospel to every creature. He that believeth and is baptized shall be saved; but he that believeth not shall be dammed. And these signs shall follow them that believe; In my name shall they cast out devils; they shall speak with new tongues; They shall take up serpents; and if they drink any deadly thing, it shall not hurt them; they shall lay hands on the sick, and they shall recover."

The Apostle Peter was given the divine power of God to heal those who were suffering from sickness and to cast out demons from those who were possessed. The Apostle Peter with the divine power and mercy of the Holy Spirit blessed many and revealed God's kindness and love for His creation.

The Apostle John was the youngest and lived the longest of the Apostles. The Apostle John's life was focused on being in the will of God and preaching the gospel of the kingdom of God and His return. He was beaten a number of times and spent time in prison for preaching the word of God.

John 7:38 reads, "He that believeth on me, as the scripture hath said, out of his belly shall flow rivers of living water."

The Apostle John had a profound relationship with Jesus and understood the importance of having the Holy Spirit direct his daily life. Jesus and the Holy Spirit transformed his personality, his values, and his heart to a man of great compassion and love for all of God's creation.

The Holy Spirit changed John the fisherman (the natural and fallen man) into a new man. The Apostle John was a man who lived for the purpose of saving souls and revealing God's plan for all of mankind. The Holy Spirit convicted John of his natural man's flaws and filled those areas with kindness and compassion for all those in need.

Jesus knew and trusted the Apostle John with the care of his mother (Mary). Jesus recognized the depth of kindness and love of the Apostle John and entrusted him as the provider for the care of Mary.

1 John 4:7–8 reads, "Beloved let us love one another: for love is of God; and every one that loveth is born of God, and knoweth God. He that loveth not knoweth not God; for God is love."

The Apostle John experienced the full meaning of love when he stood with Mary at the foot of the cross where Jesus the Christ gave His life for all. The love and kindness that is shared by each believer is the love and kindness from the Holy Spirit that indwells each believer.

The Apostle John was bold and direct in his writing and preaching in delivering the message of obeying God's commands and loving one another. This glorious Apostle continually spoke of God the Redeemer and the need to show charity for your neighbor. The Apostle John often explained that he who does not love his neighbor does not know God, for God is love. He would also speak of obeying God's commands and avoid all sin to prove your love for God.

1 John 4:20 reads, "If a man say, I love God, and hateth his brother, he is a liar: for he that loveth not his brother whom he hath seen, how can he love God whom he hath not see?"

Loving God is following His commands, glorifying and praising His name, and showing kindness to your neighbor. A believer's faith provides victory over the world and its values and allows the believer to grow in faith.

The Apostle John reminded man that to maintain a close relationship with God he must place his desires for the things of the world and his selfish desires in its proper perspective. You cannot love the world or the things of the world and also love God. You cannot have two masters you will love one and hate the other.

Message of Self Control

GOD'S TIMING, THE WHEN and how He works in our lives can be difficult to recognize and understand. However, there are times when our prayers are answered in such a powerful way that it can only be explained as the result of a miracle from God. We have a cause and effect relationship with God. When we are in His will and obedient to his word we receive blessings. When we are trusting in ourselves and disobedient to his word we experience the consequences. This relationship is subject to God's will and timing.

2 Peter 3:8 reads, "But, beloved, be not ignorant of this one thing, that one day is with the lord as a thousand years, and a thousand years as one day."

A believer has a personal relationship with their Lord and that relationship involves the continual exchange between the physical and the spiritual. God deals with each individual on an individual basis and is continually encouraging and strengthening each individual to fulfill His purpose of ministering to all of His creation.

God dealt with Moses directly, corrected him, encouraged him, and built him into a great leader that led over 600,000 people through the wilderness for 40 years. A number of individuals became angry in the Bible. However, becoming angry and losing self control or holding on to bitterness for an extended period of time can have a devastating effect on entire families, friends, and neighbors. Words spoken in anger or words spoken without compassion are words that are not forgotten and can cause permanent damage in any relationship. We need to be in prayer each day asking for God's grace, power, and mercy as we struggle to control our thoughts, emotions, and words. As we struggle with sin each day we have Jesus Christ as our example as a man who lived a life without sin.

As believers we need to be focused on the next assignment and getting prepared for the journey home. We also have the Holy Spirit that will

Message of Self Control

comfort us when we are confused or in a difficult situation. We are complex individuals with many different challenges that only God can address and provide a solution.

Jesus Christ told the Apostle Peter that he would deny him three times. The Apostle Peter assured Jesus he would never deny him. However, the night when Jesus was arrested, beaten and taken for trial; Peter became extremely fearful and lost control of his emotions and denied that he knew Jesus three times. Peter was not prepared for the reality of the arrest and had slept rather then spent time in prayer and preparation as Jesus had requested.

1 Peter 5:8 reads, "Be sober, be vigilant; because your adversary the devil, as a roaring lion, walketh about, seeking whom he may devour:"

The Apostle Peter was proclaimed to be a courageous and committed follower of Jesus, however when reality hit, Peter's fear for his life took control and Satan was the victor. The importance of prayer is paramount in our battle with the world and Satan's demons. As Peter we are weak with many frailties and we need God's strength to carry us through the many challenges we face on a daily basis.

Mark 14: 54 reads, "And Peter followed him afar off, even into the palace of the high priest: and sat with the servants, and warmed himself at the fire."

As believers we have both successes and failures as we go through many experiences throughout our lives. We cannot be bystanders warming ourselves by the fire as Peter. We as believers are commissioned to follow God's plan for our lives.

Luke 22:31–32 reads, "And the Lord said, "Simon, Simon, behold, Satan hath desired to have you, that he may sift you as wheat. But I have prayed for thee, that thy faith fail not: and when thou art converted, strengthen thy breather."

Jesus reminded Peter that Satan would like to destroy him and throw his ashes to the wind. Jesus also told Peter that he had prayed for him that his faith would be strong and he would continue to lead the Apostles.

Luke 22: 61–62 reads, "And the Lord turned, and looked upon Peter. And Peter remembered the word of the Lord, how he had said unto him, Before the cock crow, thou shalt deny me thrice. And Peter went out, and wept bitterly."

The Apostle Peter had failed miserably and he felt the entire weight of his sin as Jesus looked straight into his soul. Surely Peter must have felt his life had ended and he was of no value to any person. Satan had used fear to bring Peter to his knees in unimaginable sorrow.

God understands our frailties and shows His mercy and grace to us as He did with the Apostle Peter. Peter had spent three years with Jesus and had witnessed countless miracles and blessings. Peter had committed himself to following Jesus and was willing to defend Jesus at all costs. However, the Apostle Peter had to experience the unbelievable sorrow from his denial to understand and develop the strength to confront the issues that he was going to encounter in the rest of his ministry. Our Lord and Savior with great love and mercy will allow challenges in our lives that we may grow in strength and share that love and strength with others.

1 Peter 4:12–14 reads, "Beloved, think it not strange concerning the fiery trial which is to try you, as though some strange thing happened unto you. But rejoice, inasmuch as ye are partakers of Christ's sufferings; that, when his glory shall be revealed, ye may be glad also with exceeding joy. If ye be reproached for the name of Christ, happy are ye; for the spirit of glory and of God resteth upon you: on their part he is evil spoken of, but on your part he is glorified."

The trials we experience throughout our life are extremely valuable in molding our character and allowing us to relate to others going through those same experiences. The pain, the joy, and emotions that fill our life are an integral part of our spirit that gives us the sensitivity to appreciate and understand what others are feeling and thinking. The Holy Spirit will direct you to those people in need and will give you the words to say and in some cases tell you what part you need to accomplish.

1 John 1: 8–9 reads, "If we say that we have no sin, we deceive ourselves, and the truth is not in us. If we confess our sins, he is faithful and just to forgive us our sins, and to cleanse us from all unrighteousness."

As believers we are still natural man or fallen man. We still sin and in many cases we sin without our realizing it because of our limited understanding of God's purpose in our lives. Man's heart is desperately evil and has problems understanding the spiritual aspect of his life. As believers we are new creatures and the Holy Spirit now directs us and submits our prayers for God's blessings and strength. As believers we recognize sin and develop a sensitivity to sin and ask for forgives when we fail. We are still in a daily battle with Satan and his demons, and need to be in prayer asking for God's strength and wisdom in dealing with sin.

Message of Self Control

Ephesians 1:11–13 reads, "In whom also we have obtained an inheritance, being predestinated according to the purpose of him who worketh all things after the counsel of his own will: That we should be to the praise of his glory, who first trusted in Christ. In whom ye also trusted, after that ye heard the word of truth, the gospel of your salvation: in whom also after that ye believed, ye were sealed with that Holy Spirit of promise."

As believers we are sealed with the Holy Spirit and have the inheritance of eternal life. The Holy Spirit is the believers' advocate, protector, encourager, and acts as a guarantee of the inheritance for salvation. A believer with the assistance of the Holy Spirit continues the battle each day with sin. However, the Holy Spirit provides the believer with a greater sensitivity to sin and allows the believer the knowledge to avoid sin.

The Apostle John and the other Apostles matured greatly during the three years of ministry with Jesus and continued that maturity during their entire life. The Apostle John lost self control when he asked Jesus to burn a Samaritan village to the ground for not welcoming Jesus on his travels through the village. Jesus rebuked the disciples and said he came to save man and not destroy man.

Luke 9:54–56 reads, "And when his disciples James and John saw this, they said, Lord, wilt thou that we command fire to come down from heaven, and consume them, even as Elijah did? But he turned, and rebuked them, and said, Ye know not what manner of spirit ye are of. For the Son of man is not come to destroy man's lives, but to save them. And they went to another village."

James and John (Sons of Thunder) were brothers who both became extremely angry and lost control of their emotions and wanted God to bring down fire from the heavens to destroy this Samaritan village.

Proverbs 14:29 reads, "He that is slow to wrath is of great understanding: but he that is hasty of spirit exalteth folly."

A person that is impatient and loses control of their temper will suffer the consequences in some way. As believers we struggle daily against principalities, against powers, and against wickedness. One of Satan's and his demon's priorities is to prevent you from accomplishing God's will for your life. God has a plan for your life and Satan will do everything he can do to prevent you from fulfilling that plan. If you find yourself consumed by anger you need take time before you respond and do or say something that you will later regret. It is important that we do not get distracted from God's plan for our lives and return to God's will as soon as possible.

The Apostle John spoke of self control and the importance of not loving the things of the world. An idol is anything that consumes our time and energy and takes the place of God. Idols can be the love of possessions, money, recognition, and many more things that hold a greater value or a priority than the worship of God. A non-believer is enslaved to sin and the worship of idols, Satan and his demons. A person who is a believer has the Holy Spirit living in their life and has broken Satan's shackles.

1 John 2:15–17 reads, "Love not the world, neither the things that are in the world. If any man love the world, the love of the father is not in him. For all that is in the world, the lust of the flesh, and the lust of the eyes, and the pride of life, is not of the Father, but is of the world. And the world passeth away, and the lust thereof: but he that doeth the will of God abideth for ever."

A person who loves Jesus Christ and follows God's commandments will break free of the sins of the world, its' idols and commune with the Holy Spirit. The Holy Spirit allows the believer to take control of his life and start to live a life that is focused on pleasing God and spending his time and energy helping others.

Psalm 119: 11–16 reads, "Thy word have I hid in mine heart, that I might not sin against thee. Blessed art thou, O Lord: teach me thy statutes. With my lips have I declared all the judgments of thy mouth. I have rejoiced in the way of thy testimonies, as much as in all riches. I will meditate in thy precepts, and have respect unto thy ways. I will delight myself in thy statutes: I will not forget thy word."

The believer is able to take on greater understanding and appreciation of God's word as he spends more time in meditation.

Message of the Law

THE MESSAGE OF THE law begins with God and His delivery of the law through Jesus, Moses and the prophets. Jesus told all of mankind that He had come to fulfill the law.

Matthew 5:17 reads, "Think not that I am come to destroy the law, or the prophets: I am not come to destroy, but to fulfill."

In Genesis God reveals His plan for both men and women.

Genesis 2:24 reads, "Therefore shall a men leave his father and his mother, and shall cleave unto his wife: and they shall be one flesh."

God created man and woman for a number of reasons. Their marriage is a sacred bond that is blessed by God for the purpose raising a family and instructing their children in God's teachings. This marriage of a man and woman is a union of mutual love, honor, respect and support. The Apostle Paul in his letter to the church of Thessalonica addressed some of the struggles found within the church.

1 Thessalonians 4:3-5 reads, "For this is the will of God, even your sanctification, that ye should abstain from fornication: That every one of you should know how to possess his vessel in sanctification and honor; Not in the lust of concupiscence, even as the Gentiles which know not God."

We are to control and prevent sin from contaminating our marriages or our bodies (vessels) that God has given us. The early church struggled with many issues found in a pagan society. Any monies related to these pagan practices were not allowed in God's holy church.

Deuteronomy 23:17-18 reads, "There shall be no whore of the daughters of Israel, nor a sodomite of the sons of Israel. Thou shalt not bring the hire of a whore, or the price of a dog, into the house of the Lord thy God for any vow: for even both these are abomination unto the Lord thy God."

Society was infested with many pagan practices that would attack and blame the Christians for any natural disaster that may occur. Christians were viewed as a threat by many persons who were benefiting financially from these pagan practices. No member of the local pagan society or any related funds were allowed into the house of the Lord.

God sent His angels to both Joseph and Mary to ensure this sacred bond of marriage would be complete and perfect under the law. The birth of Jesus created a sacred bond between God and man, and would allow Jesus to live a life as a man and take on the sins of all of mankind. Jesus took on the form of a man and lived as a man without sin to be the perfect sacrifice for all of man's sin. Jesus was both God and man and His life would bridge the gap between sin and heaven.

Exodus 20:1–17 reads, "And God spake all these words, saying. I am the Lord they God, which have brought thee out of the land of Egypt, out of the house of bondage. Thou shall have no other gods before me. Thou shalt not make unto thee any graven image, or any likeness of any thing that is in heaven above, or that is in the earth beneath, or that is in the water under the earth. Thou shalt not bow down thyself to them, nor serve them: for I the Lord thy God am a jealous God, visiting the iniquity of the fathers upon the children unto the third and fourth generation of them that hate me; And showing mercy unto thousands of them that love me, and keep my commandments. Thou shalt not take the name of the Lord thy God in vain: for the Lord will not hold him guiltless that taketh his name in vain. Remember the Sabbath day, to keep it holy. Six days shalt thou labor, and do all thy work: But the seventh day is the Sabbath of the Lord thy God: in it thou shalt not do any work, thou, nor thy son, nor thy daughter, thy manservant, nor thy maidservant, nor thy cattle, nor thy stranger that is within thy gates. For in six days the Lord made heaven and earth, the sea, and all that in them is, and rested the seventh day, wherefore the Lord blessed the sabbath day, and hallowed it. Honor thy father and thy mother: that thy days maybe long upon the land which the Lord thy God giveth thee. Thou shalt not kill. Thou shalt not commit adultery. Thou shalt not steal. Thou shalt not bear false witness against the neighbor. Thou shalt not covet thy neighbor's house, thou shalt not covet thy neighbor's wife, nor his manservant, nor his maidservant, nor his ox, nor his ass, nor any thing that is thy neighbor's."

These commandments begin with loving the Lord your God with all your heart, soul, and mind. God should hold the most important position in your life and be your first priority in any decision. Our very existence on this planet is only possible with God's grace and love. We are commanded not to bow down or serve any other God. Another god would be anything you consider to be more important than worshiping God.

We are commanded not to take the Lord's name in vain. We are only allowed to come to God in prayer because of His merciful love and endless grace. Any man who brings dishonor or uses God's name in vain will experience His holy retribution. We are to honor and praise God at every opportunity.

God created the heavens and the earth in six days and rested on the seventh. God requires us to set aside the Sabbath as a day to remember what He has done for us and keep it holy. He gave His only Son that we may live for eternity with Him. Our focus on the Sabbath is to thank God for all His blessings and to sing praises to His holy name.

Honor your father and mother is a commandment from God. One honors their father and mother in many ways. The family is an extremely important unit in our society and is directly related to how well society functions in addressing many different laws, rules and opinions. A child that is not taught to respect and honor their father and mother will not respect the laws and rules of society.

Thou shalt not kill is a commandment that is difficult to explain. At first brush, it seems it would be simple to explain. However, we have many individuals that are often required to kill while serving in the military or in a law enforcement position. In the case of the military, the killing of individuals is required to protect and prevent the killing of innocent men, women, and children. History records many wars and battles that were fought for many different reasons. Generally, governments are in control of deciding if a declaration of war is approved and killings are justified. Law enforcement officers take an oath to protect the citizens of a state or country and are given the authority to use deadly force if necessary. Using deadly force is only used when all other options have been exhausted. However, there are always exceptions to the rule and that would include intent. Some individuals, solely on their own volition will plan and kill another individual for money, revenge, pride, and many other sinful reasons. Today, these acts are generally referred to a premeditated murder.

Thou shalt not commit adultery is a commandment that is an extremely serious sin that has been responsible for countless numbers of marriages ending over thousands of years. Adultery is a sin that occurs within a marriage between a man and women. Adultery is committed when a man or the women is unfaithful to the sacred marriage bond. The reason why this

God's Messengers

sin is so common today is because of lack of moral standards and in some cases the actual promotion of pagan practices too perverse to describe.

Stealing of goods and property is a common sin today that occurs throughout the world. Stealing would include corruption and other methods to defraud or cheat people out of the money or property. In some countries today, corruption is so prevalent that laws are seldom enforced by local authorities. There are some groups that believe they are entitled to whatever they wish. These individuals will actually kill another individual if they possess something they wish. King David was guilty of this sin and many others.

To bear false witness against your neighbor is to tell a lie. Man has a fallen nature and will lie for any number of different reasons in many different situations. Many have been convinced by the evil one (the great liar) that lying is not a sin. Lying is a very powerful tool that can bring great harm to any person in many different ways. Lying is so prevalent today that it is very difficult to determine the truth from a lie.

Exodus 23:1–3 reads, "Thou shalt not raise a false report: put not thine hand with the wicked to be an unrighteous witness. Thou shalt not follow a multitude to do evil: neither shalt thou speak in a cause to decline after many to wrest judgment. Neither shalt thou countenance a poor man in his cause."

As Christians we need to realize Satan is the great liar and is working feverously to destroy as many lives as possible. God commanded man to love God with all his heart, soul and mind. God also commanded man to love his neighbor as himself. King David loved his son Solomon and directed him to keep all of God's commandments and statutes to unsure he would have good success.

1 Kings 2:3 reads, "And keep the charge of the Lord thy God, to walk in his ways, to keep his statutes, and his commandments, and his judgments, and his testimonies, as it is written in the law of Moses, that thou mayest prosper in all that thou doest, and whithersoever thou turnest thyself."

Jesus told all of mankind that if they loved Him they needed to obey His commandments and statutes.

John 14:15–16 reads, "If ye love me, keep my commandents. And I will pray the Father, and he shall give you another Comforter, that he may abide with you for ever."

In addition to the commandments God has provided many rules and statutes that a believers needs to follow and apply to their daily lives.

Ephesians 4:19 reads, "Who being past feeling have given themselves over unto lasciviousness, to work all uncleanness with greediness"

Some men have fallen so deep into depravity that they are no longer able to distinguish moral right from wrong. Today, society has fallen to a great depth of moral decay where perversion is celebrated.

Ephesians: 4:22 reads, "That ye put off concerning the former conversation the old man, which is corrupt according to the deceitful lusts."

A new believer takes on a new character and must identify and repent of their sins. A new believer is convicted by the Holy Spirit of the sin in their lives and must bury the old desires, values, and temptations. Lusts of the flesh must be eliminated and new interests must be cultivated.

Ephesians 4:29-30 reads, "Let no corrupt communication proceed out of your mouth, but that which is good to the use of edifying, that it may minister grace unto the hearers. And grieve not the holy Spirit of God, whereby ye are sealed unto the day of redemption."

We need to be careful about the words we use on a daily basis. Do we speak out of love and concern for our neighbor's well-being? Is our language guided by the Holy Spirit? We need to run from evil and not be swallowed up by evil pressures and temptations. Today's society and its values are full of evil and those that are trying to convince man that there is nothing wrong with today's morals

Justice for mankind is based on truth. Christians should not be involved in or in some way associated with a persons or organizations that use lies or false reports to discredit people.

Conclusion

God uses many different people, angels, and circumstances to deliver messages to Christians on a daily basis. In the past God used certain angels to deliver messages depending on the importance of the message. For example, the archangel Gabriel was sent by God to Daniel to help him with the interpretation of visions. These visions spoke of the coming of the Messiah, the forgiveness of sins and the hope of salvation. The archangel Gabriel was also used to deliver a message to Mary and Joseph that Mary would give birth to Jesus Christ, God's only Son. Certainly, the birth of God's Son and the Savior of mankind would require an archangel to make the announcement. The archangel Gabriel was also used by God to deliver a message to Zechariah that his elderly wife Elizabeth would deliver a baby and his name would be John the Baptist. The birth of John the Baptist was another important announcement due to his relationship to Jesus and the fact he would prepare the way for Jesus' ministry. The importance of Jesus' baptism cannot be overstated since God himself said in Matthew 3:17, "And lo a voice from heaven, saying, this is my beloved Son, in whom I am well pleased."

It is believed that a myriad (too many to count) of angels were created by God before the earth's creation. These angels fulfill a number of tasks from protecting Christians, providing comfort to the sick, watching over children, battling Satan and his demons, delivering messages, and worshiping and praising God for his endless love and grace. Angels were also created in different forms. For example, a Seraphim is an angel with six wings with two wings that cover his feet, two wings cover his face, and two wings for flying. A Seraphim is a caretaker for God's throne.

Angels have been seen by many as they deliver messages from God to his faithful servants. Abraham saw two angels standing outside of his tent one day. They told Abraham of the pending destruction of Sodom and

Gomorra because of their depravity and sinfulness. After some begging by Abraham, God allowed the angels to escort Lot and his family out of the city under one condition. They were to leave the city without turning back. Lot's wife turned back and was turned into a pillar of salt. Obviously, Lot's wife was deeply in love with the people of Sodom and Gomorra and could not say no to her desires and love of wickedness. Today, our society has accepted evil practices and depravity as acceptable behavior and has passed laws that protect those who are engaged in these evil practices.

God also delivers messages to His faithful in the form of dreams. Joseph was able to interpret dreams and relayed God's messages to the Pharaoh. This gift resulted in Joseph becoming a leader in Egypt and rescuing his family. King Solomon communicated with God in a dream that resulted in Solomon receiving great wisdom and understanding in leading the people of Israel. Daniel through God was able to interpret a dream for King Nebuchadnezzar. Jacob's dream of a ladder was a representation of Jesus as the perfect ladder between man and God.

God communicates with man throughout his entire life. He stands at the door of each man's heart waiting for man to invite Him in and receive the gift of salvation. He may use a number of different methods to communicate with man. God may communicate with man through a Bible study and prayer, through a pastor or another person, or through a song or book. He may allow a situation to be used as an example for a personal application. God may use a dream to communicate an opportunity or problem that needs to be addressed or resolved. The avenues for communication with God are endless and needs to be studied and reviewed under careful consideration.

Man was born into sin and must walk in the Spirit to be able to reject the desires of the flesh and have victory over all temptations. God has given us the power to say no to any of Satan's temptations and sins.

God is able to look into the heart of a person and determine if that person will grow in faith and be obedient to God's word. These are generally men that have grown in great humility and have fallen at God's feet in worship. God looked at these men not for who they are or were, but for what they would become.

1 Samuel 16:7 reads, "But the Lord said unto Samuel, Look not on his countenance, or on the height of the stature; because I have refused him: for the Lord seeth not as man seeth; for man looketh on the outward appearance, but the Lord looketh on the heart."

God's Messengers

God's Spirit indwelled these men and communed with their hearts and souls. From the beginning of creation the Holy Spirit has been actively comforting, convicting, and blessing those that have been anointed by faith.

Genesis 1:2 reads, "And the earth was without form, and void: and darkness was upon the face of the deep. And the Spirit of God moved upon the face of the waters."

God created this glorious and wonderful earth for us to care for and enjoy. He also created men and women that they may experience God's blessings and grow in appreciation of all what life has to offer.

God is a loving God that wants all people to spend eternity with Him and to experience all of His grace, mercy, and blessings. However, to experience God's grace, mercy, and blessings for eternity one must place God first in their life and place all of their trust and faith in Him. The believers that have crossed over or will cross over the bridge built on the death of God's only Son, Jesus Christ will experience blessings too numerous to count and will be able to rejoice as they never have rejoiced before.

God's plan for mankind started at the beginning. The unfolding of God's plan involved God selecting men that would carry great responsibility at specific points in time. Life is a precious gift from God that is for all of mankind. This life is short and fragile and can be shortened further by disease, accidents, and any number of other circumstances. At first glance, it is difficult to understand why millions of people refuse to believe in Jesus and His message of salvation. Unfortunately, one reason for this refusal is related to many Christians that are only Christians on Sunday. This hypocrisy is seen by the common man and either delays or prevents any further consideration for making a decision to investigate Christianity. Another obstacle for making a decision to accept Christ is the heart of the common man and his love of sin. He or she may love and worship any number of pagan gods. As discussed early, man worships the same pagan gods as he did during the time of Elijah and Moses. The names may have changed from Baal to wealth, or Asherah to pleasure, but the idea has remained the same. Anything that stands between you and God or prevents you from worshiping God is a sin. Millions of people are not Christians and many have no desire to become a Christian. The result will be that only believers will be able to share eternity with their Creator.

God transformed Moses into one of the worlds' greatest leaders and laid on him great responsibilities. Moses' life started as a baby adopted by the Pharaohs' daughter and was denied nothing during his childhood. He

CONCLUSION

was given the best education but was conflicted about his place in life. Moses loved the Israelites and killed one of the Pharaoh's guards at the age of 40 and fled for his life. He spent the next 40 years in the wilderness herding sheep and hiding from the Egyptian rule.

God found Moses in the wilderness as a sheep herder with many weaknesses, no confidence, and living in fear. God was able to change him into one of God's greatest messengers. God gave Moses tremendous courage that allowed him to stand in front of the Pharaoh and demand that he release the Israelites from bondage.

Numbers 12:3 reads, "Now the man Moses was very meek, above all the men which were upon the face of the earth."

Psalm 103:7 reads, "He made know his ways unto Moses, his acts unto the children of Israel."

Moses was not only meek, he was the meekest of all men. God needed a man that He could use and mold into a great leader and be obedient to His commandments. All believers will experience God's mercy as He develops in each man faith and humility. We all struggle with the natural man and his love of self. We are all on a journey that requires of us to grow in faith, obedience and in humility as we pray and open God's word and fill our souls with His love, mercy, and His direction. We are all like Moses in that we struggle with life and are not always open to God's direction.

Moses was transformed into God's messenger. Moses was the man that God wanted to lead the Israelites out of Egypt and out from under slavery.

Deuteronomy 34:10-12 reads, "And there arose not a prophet since in Israel like unto Moses, whom the Lord knew face to face. In all the signs and the wonders, which the Lord sent him to do in the land of Egypt to Pharaoh, and to all his servants, and to all his land. And in all that mighty hand and in all the great terror which Moses showed in the sight of all Israel."

God transformed Moses to be the man to mark a new beginning and to fulfill the promise to Abraham to make Israel a great nation.

Elijah was a "Tishbite," a Hebrew name meaning My God is Yahweh. As Moses, Elijah spent a great deal of the time in the wilderness surviving off the land. Elijah was a little known priest and prophet that managed to survive by living in caves with nothing other than the clothes on his back.

Elijah was also a messenger and prophet of God and was very bold and courageous as he challenged the people to decide between God and

Baal. Elijah prophesied that there would be three years of severe drought that would cause catastrophic harm to the country and its people.

God spoke through Elijah at a critical point in time. The people of Israel in the Northern Kingdom under King Ahab and Queen Jezebel were being forced to worship Baal and other pagan gods. Queen Jezebel was a devote follower of the pagan gods and demanded that all the people worship these gods of stone. To resist or disobey this command could be met with death or severe punishment.

Elijah was a faithful prophet of God and a man that was completely dependent on God for direction and his daily needs. Elijah was not only obedient to God's direction, but he acted without fear as he approached King Ahab and demanded that he allow the people to worship the true God. As Moses, Elijah was a man that God talked to directly and indwelled his entire being. Both Moses and Elijah had many frailties and failed on many occasions.

1Kings 18:1 reads, "And it came to pass after many days, that the word of the Lord came to Elijah in the third year, saying, Go, show thyself unto Ahab, and I will send rain upon the earth."

However, God was able to use these men because of their humble spirits and souls and their obedience to God's word regardless of the dangers. Both of these men with God's strength were able to face evil and ruthless rulers without being executed and make demands sighting God's commands.

The Apostle James, another one of God's messengers is recognized as the first Apostle to be martyred for his belief in the gospel. It is at this point in time that marks the beginning when many of the Apostles would be martyred for their faith and their willingness to preach the word of God regardless of the consequences. The Apostle James' death and martyrdom is a reflection of Jesus Christ's Crucifixion and the challenge that Jesus gave to James and John when they agreed to drink from His cup.

Mark 10: 37-38 reads, "They said unto him, Grant unto us that we may sit, one on the right hand, and the other on thy left hand, in thy glory. But Jesus said unto them, "Ye know not what ye ask: can ye drink of the cup that I drink of? and be baptized with that baptism that I am baptized with?"

We are all natural men with limited understanding of God's love, mercy, glory, and plans. We have no concept of the sorrow and suffering that Jesus Christ had to endure from the wrath of God for sins of all mankind. We think and apply our own understanding, desires, and wishes to God's

CONCLUSION

plan for all of mankind. We ask for things as natural man that is selfish and is not in keeping with God's spiritual plan for our life.

The Apostle James was one of the first and oldest of the Apostles and in some ways the most mature. When Jesus asked James (the greater) to follow him he did not hesitate to say yes. He was bold in his speaking and fearless in his approach to witnessing of the life and death of Jesus Christ his Savior. Jesus the Christ came into this world as a humble servant and as a man who revealed His love by healing thousands and explaining the way of salvation.

Isaiah 53: 3-6 reads, "He is despised and rejected of men; a man of sorrows, and acquainted with grief: and we hid as it were our faces from him; he was despised, and we esteemed him not. Surely he hath borne our griefs, and carried our sorrows: yet we did esteem him stricken, smitten of God, and afflicted. But he was wounded for our transgressions, he was bruised for our iniquities: the chastisement of our peace was upon him; and with his stripes we are healed. All we like sheep have gone astray; we have turned every one to his own way; and the Lord hath laid on him the iniquity of us all."

Jesus came to this earth and lived his life as a humble servant as our example as to how to love our neighbor. As Moses and Elijah, James was a humble man of God. The Apostle James (the greater) was courageous and continued to preach fiery sermons (son of thunder) knowing the temple priests were plotting his demise. Eventually, King Herod arrested him and killed him with a sword to the pleasure of the people. It is believed that the Apostle James approached his death singing the glories of his Savior.

The Apostle Peter was a very humble man and sensitive to those around him.

Luke 5:8 reads, "When Simon Peter saw it, he fell down at Jesus' knees, saying, Depart from me; for I am a sinful man, O Lord."

The Apostle Peter quickly realized that he was in the presence of God and that his life was full of sin. Peter's heart and soul were aware of God's presence and he had to humble himself at Jesus' feet to show respect and to plea for mercy. It was Peter who first recognized Jesus as His Savior and Lord.

Mathew 16:16 reads, "And Simon Peter answered and said, Thou art the Christ, the Son of the living God."

As Peter, we need to respect and humble ourselves in the presence of our Lord and Savior, Jesus the Christ, the Son of God.

God's Messengers

Mathew 16:17-18 reads, "And Jesus answered and said unto him, "Blessed art thou, Simon Bar-jona: for flesh and blood hath not revealed it unto thee, but my Father which is in heaven. And I say also thee, That thou art Peter and upon this rock I will build my church: and the gates of hell shall not prevail against it."

At this point in time we see another part of God's plan unfold for mankind as God tells Peter he will use him as a foundation for building His Church. This is a great honor and an unspeakable privilege and a great responsibility for the Apostle Peter.

The Apostle Peter was a common man that made many mistakes, but God was patient and corrected him in love many times. From God's patient loving care the Apostle Peter grew in wisdom and understanding of what was required to be a servant.

Luke 5:10 reads, "And so was also James, and John, the sons of Zebedee, which were partners with Simon. And Jesus said unto Simon, Fear not; from henceforth thou shalt catch men."

The Apostles James, John, and Peter were all summoned by Jesus to be fishers of men. They were all in God's presence and they were all going to be trained by Jesus (the Son of God) to be servants to God's word.

The Apostle John was the youngest of the early Apostles and was the only Apostle that died of natural causes. The Apostle John was called by Jesus as the beloved disciple and was at present at most of the miracles.

John 21: 20-23 reads, "Then Peter, turning about, seeth the disciple whom Jesus loved following; which also leaned on his breast at supper, and said, Lord, which is he that betrayeth thee? Peter seeing him saith to Jesus, Lord, and what shall this man do? Jesus saith unto him, If I will that he tarry till I come what is that to thee? follow thou me."

Jesus refused to tell the Apostle Peter God's plan for the Apostle John's life. God's plan for the Apostle John was not known to any man. No man knows God's plan for any man. God's plan for each individual varies as different as each man's character.

The Apostle John learned from Jesus and grew to be a messenger who was willing to suffer and sacrifice all for the gospel. He understood that humility was paramount if he was going to achieve any success in building the church through God. The Apostle John patiently suffered at Patmos where he lived in a cave for years.

The Apostle John was also passionate in his proclamation of the gospel and willingness to defend the truth. John also learned from Jesus

Conclusion

his strong love for others and grew in humility as the church was blessed and grew. The Apostle John understood the importance of humility and to guard against the constant threat of self and pride. His passion for the truth and his compassion to be a servant was always paramount.

Moses as God's messenger fulfilled God's promise to bring his people to the Promised Land. God's messenger, Elijah turned God's people from worshiping pagan gods to worshiping the one true God. James life as God's messenger marked the beginning of the martyrdom of the Apostles. Peter's life laid the foundation for delivering God's message for the church and salvation. John's long life as God's messenger was to identify the church as a loving extension of Jesus Christ for all of mankind. These messengers represented God's plan for all of mankind, from the promise made to Abraham of a Promised Land to the book of Revelation written by the Apostle John.

John 1:14 reads, "And the Word was made flesh, and dwelt among us, and we beheld his glory, the glory as of the only begotten of the Father, full of grace and truth."

All of God's messengers were obedient to God's word, courageous with God's strength, and assumed great responsibilities in God's plan. They all understood that they were servants and were required to deliver God's message of love and salvation to all of mankind.

Luke 9:46–48 reads, "Then there arose a reasoning among them, which of them should be greatest. And Jesus, perceiving the thought of their heart, took a child, and set him by him. And said unto them, whoever shall receive this child in my name receiveth me: and whosoever shall receive me receiveth him that sent me: for he that is least among you all, the same shall be great."

Jesus Christ came to this earth not as a king but as a servant to save those that were lost in their sin. Following Jesus and obeying God's commands requires one to be a servant to others. God's messengers were servants to all of mankind and understood they were servants to all of those they lead by following God's direction in mercy, grace, and love. They were humble servants that patiently waited on God for direction.

As believers we are transformed from being a self-centered individual to a person that places Jesus Christ as our center. We grow in maturity as we become more obedient and are challenged to accept more responsibilities. Our relationship with God evolves as he sees we are trustworthy and able to accomplish spiritual tasks.

God's Messengers

God's messengers have always delivered a message that becoming a Christian is a lifelong process of living as a servant to others with the leading and strength of the Holy Spirit.

Romans 12:1–3 reads, "I beseech you therefore, brethren, by the mercies of God, that ye present your bodies a living sacrifice, holy, acceptable unto God, which is your reasonable service. And be not conformed to this world: but be ye transformed by the renewing of your mind, that ye may prove what is that good, and acceptable, and perfect, will of God. For I say, through the grace given unto you, to every man that is among you, not to think of himself more highly then he ought to think; but to think soberly, according as God hath dealt to every man the measure of faith."

As believers we are in a process of transforming our lives from one of being self-centered and living as a natural man to one of surrendering and submitting our lives to serving others. Moses was a humble servant of God who led the Israelites to the Promised Land. Elijah was the humble servant that God used to destroy the worship of pagan gods and return Israel to the worship of the one true God. James was the humble servant who gave his life for the furtherance of the gospel. Peter was the humble servant that God used as a foundation for the church. John was the humble servant that was used by God to build the church and deliver God's word. Their wisdom, courage, strength, obedience, and loving kindness were a reflection of God in their lives and His plan for all of mankind. God the Almighty is loving and merciful, full of grace, faithful, and patience to all of mankind.

God sent His only Son to become a man, a humble servant, and to be obedient to His word even unto death on the cross.

Philippians 2:8–11 reads, "And being found in fashion as a man, he humbled himself, and became obedient unto death, even death on the cross. Wherefore God also hath highly exalted him, and given him a name which is above every name. That at the name of Jesus every knee should bow, of things in heaven, and things in earth, and things under the earth; And that every tongue should confess that Jesus Christ is Lord, to the glory of God the Father."

We have been given example after example of how to live as a humble servant. As believers we are being transformed from the natural man to the spiritual man. This lifelong process will end as we are all transfigured into another form as our faces begin to shine brightly, as our lives begin to become more like our Savior and Lord, and as we begin to sing praises to our Creator.

Conclusion

We have limited understanding of the mind of God and His ways. However, after reading and studying the Bible we can grasp some basic commands and principles. God is extremely patient, loving and offers salvation to all that will obey His commands and statutes.

Ephesians 2:8-9 reads, "For by grace are ye save through faith; and that not of yourselves: it is the gift of God: Not of works, lest any man should boast"

Ephesians 3:16-19 reads, "That he would grant you, according to the riches of glory, to be strengthened with might by his Spirit in the inner man; That Christ may dwell in your hearts by faith; that ye, being rooted and grounded in love, May be able to comprehend with all saints what is the breadth, and length, and depth, and height; And to know the love of Christ, which passeth knowledge, that ye might be filled with all the fullness of God."

Colossians 3:12 reads, "Put on therefore, as the elect of God, holy and beloved, bowels of mercies, kindness, humbleness of mind, meekness, long-sufferings."

Throughout history man has been born into many different situations and circumstances. Some have been born into great wealth and some were born into dire poverty. Some have been able to take advantage of many opportunities and some have never traveled more than hundred miles from their place of birth. Some have been given every opportunity to grow into becoming great athletes and others have severe physical limitations. Some are born with great mental abilities and are blessed with many talents and others struggle with the daily challenges of life.

God created each person as a unique individual with a unique purpose in life. Some are able to identify God's purpose for their life in a short amount of time and others struggle to find that purpose for many years. God's plan for mankind is a perfect plan and uses each person's talents and gifts at the appropriate time.

All of mankind started with Adam and his wife Eve. They were made in the image of God and would be part of God's plan in populating the entire world for all of mankind.

Genesis 3:20 reads, "And Adam called his wife's name Eve; because she was the mother of all living."

Today we see many people with many different types of characteristics, but they still all belong to the same human race. Many of these differences resulted from God's plan for man. It is believed that God forced man to migrate, become subject to different environments, experience isolation, develop different languages, live on different diets, and to live under many other influences. Man's sin and his defiance against God in the building of the Tower of Babel caused God to bring blindness and confusion of speech to the people at the time.

Isaiah 46:10–11 reads, "Declaring the end from the beginning, and from ancient times the things that are not yet done, saying, My counsel shall stand, and I will do all my pleasure: Calling a ravenous bird from the east, the man that executeth my counsel from a far country: yea, I have spoken it, I will also bring it to pass; I have purposed it, I will also do it."

God is incomprehensible and He knows all from the beginning to the end.

Jeremiah 1:5 reads, "Before I formed thee in the belly I knew thee; and before thou camest forth out of the womb I sanctified thee, and I ordained thee a prophet unto the nations."

God knew Jeremiah before he was born. God knows us all and gives us the freedom to make the decision to accept or reject His love.

Man has established laws and rules designed to protect him from himself. Man has a fallen character that allows for sin to exist and grow in his daily life. Satan is the great liar and takes advantage of man's weakness by tempting him with many rewards. These rewards could be popularity, status, wealth, acceptance, career opportunities, and many more socially approved goals. Throughout history society has placed a great deal of pressure on the Christian to conform to its morals and ethics. Many evil kings and rulers have passed laws that have required Christians to worship idols and other pagan practices. Many Christians have refused to conform over history and have been martyred for their Christian beliefs. Satan is the great liar, deceiver, and murderer. He has convinced millions of women to kill their innocent babies. He has convinced millions of children and adults that there is nothing wrong with sexual perversion.

There is a direct relationship between sin and discipline. The world will continue to suffer God's wrath as more laws are passed that disobeys God's commandments.

Proverbs 6:16–19 reads, "These six things doth the Lord hate; yea, seven are an abomination unto him: A proud look, a lying tongue, and hands that shed innocent blood. A heart that deviseth wicked imaginations, feet that be swift in running to mischief, A false witness that speaketh lies, and he that soweth discord among brethren."

CONCLUSION

Some of the pagan and the most egregious sins are not mentioned due to the fact they are not allowed to be spoken, written or repeated. God will reject those people that are self absorbed, arrogant, and insensitive to others. He will reject those that deliberately deceive others or cause harm to others with their lies. God will hold those accountable that are involved in the taking of innocent blood or abortion. God will reject those that have allowed their minds to be involved in the forming of wicked imaginations. Those that are involved in scheming to cause harm to others will be rejected. Speaking lies or bearing false witness will be rejected. God hates those that cause strife or creates distrust.

We all need to take an honest evaluation of the message we are sending to our loved ones and our neighbors. It is also important to realize that evil has a great deal of influence over what we hear and see on a daily basis. If at all possible we need to avoid evil and not to be entrapped into some never ending debate over good and evil. We rest in God's inerrant word the Bible and place all of our understanding in God's love and grace. We are all sinners and are subject to our fallen nature. We are at war with evil each day and we live in faith under the protection of our Lord and Savior.

We are all messengers in Gods' plan. The message is that God loves the world and that He has freely given His only Son. Those that believe in His Son, Jesus Christ will be given eternal life. Man is no longer forced to worship the pagan gods. We no longer see the massive temples that were built to worship the pagan gods of Greece and Rome. We no longer see the hundreds of pagan priests that required man to make sacrifices to appease the pagan gods. However, some of the pagan practices and rituals of the past still survive today.

Today the need is great for those that are God's messengers.

Today we see the results of a society that has failed to provide basic moral values. We see generation after generation of children left alone to wander the streets without any parental guidance. Many of these children drop out of school at early age and begin a life of crime in order to survive. To stop this vicious cycle of crime and violence society needs to make some major changes. Children that are at risk need to be indentified at an early age and closely mentored until such time they are productive members of society. This is one area that has been ignored for many years due to many different reasons. Both State and federal agencies with limited funding has struggled for years to meet this critical need. This situation is now out of control to where young children are involved in serious crimes daily in most cities.

Christians, the church, and the family are under attack from Satan and his demons from every direction. Children are being attacked at their schools and being forced to read and learn about pagan practices. Schools are teaching children that there is no God, no creator, and no divine plan and purpose for their lives. Satan and his demons are using every possible method to undermine and discredit the family. Divorce is an easy and common solution used today to resolve any disagreement in a marriage. The result is millions are children are left without the love and support of a father and mother. Satan and his demons are attacking the church in many different ways. The church for years has not been taxed due to it's work of providing food and shelter for the poor for the world. Now governments are threatening to disallow this tax emption if churches do not comply with new government rules and regulations.

In some ways not a lot has changed since Jesus and His disciples walked on this earth 2000 years ago. Jesus threw the money changers out of the temple for cheating the poor and turning the Lord's house of worship into a corrupt place of business. Many churches today have lost their way and are focused on fund raising and not saving souls. The Apostle John and Paul were beaten and imprisoned for preaching the gospel of Jesus Christ and exposing the corruption at the pagan temples. Rome had built a number of temples to establish control and to force their captives to pay taxes, to worship Caesar and many other pagan gods. The Christian church and it's preaching were viewed by the pagans and their government as a threat to their business of selling pagan rituals. Those that attended the Christian church and made a decision to believe in Jesus realized that they needed to follow God's commandments. They stopped their worship of the pagan gods and stopped the payment to the corrupt temple priests for making sacrifices to the pagan gods. The early followers of Apostle John and Paul learned that Jesus paid the price for all of their sins and there was no longer any need to make sacrifices to the pagan gods. The early believers were beaten for not participating in the pagan practices and not worshiping at the pagan temples. The old temples have disappeared except for a few ruins, but some pagan practices still exist today. Satan (the great liar) and his demons will not give up trying to destroy the Christian church and it's believers.

Conclusion

God loves us and is always available to hear our concerns and wishes. God communicates with us in a number of different ways. He may use the Holy Spirit to guide us, angels to lead us, dreams to instruct us, nature to reveal His beauty and power, a pillar of fire to direct us, Jesus to comfort us, and prophets and the Bible for revelation.

God spoke to Adam and Eve in the garden.

Genesis 3:8 reads, "And they heard the voice of the Lord God walking in the garden in the cool of the day: and Adam and his wife hid themselves from the presence of the Lord God amongst the trees of the garden. And the Lord God called unto Adam, and said unto him, Where are thou?"

God loved Adam and Eve and called out to them with concern. Even though Adam and Eve sinned God still clothed them. God is always there searching for us even when we are lost deep in sin. His love is never ending.

Jesus instructed us to seek first the kingdom of God.

Matthew 6:33 reads, "Bur seek ye first the kingdom of God, and his righteousness; and all these things shall be added unto you."

Jesus' message to mankind is clear; we are instructed to continually seek after God's kingdom and His righteousness. As Christians our first priority is to worship God and to trust God for any material needs. God will provide for us and we are instructed not to worry about tomorrow.

The Holy Spirit was sent by Jesus to provide a message of peace and comfort. The Holy Spirit communicates continually to the Christian each day and in many different ways.

John 14:26-27 reads, "But the Comforter, which is the Holy Ghost, whom the Father will send in my name, he shall teach you all things, and bring all things to your remembrance, whatsoever I have said unto you. Peace I leave with you, my peace I give unto you: not as the world giveth, give I unto you. Let not your heart be troubled, neither let it be afraid."

The Christian has a very unique and wonderful relationship with the Holy Spirit. The Holy Spirit is extremely powerful and is able to bring great peace and comfort to the Christian. The God that raised Jesus from the dead is the same the same God and Holy Spirit that lives within the Christian. (Romans 8:11)

Angels surround us to form a barrier to protect us.

Psalm 103:19-20 reads, "The Lord hath prepared his throne in the heavens; and his kingdom ruleth over all. Bless the Lord, ye his angels, that excel in strength, that do his commandments, hearkening unto the voice of his word."

God's Messengers

Psalm 34:7 reads, "The angel of the Lord encampeth round about them that fear him, and delivereth them."

2 Kings 6:17 reads, "And Elisha prayed, and said, Lord, I pray thee, open his eyes, that he may see. And the Lord opened the eyes of the young man; and he saw: and, behold, the mountain was full of horses and chariots of fire round about Eliaha."

Hebrews 1:14 reads, "Are they not all ministering spirits, sent forth to minister for them who shall be heirs of salvation."

The angels were created by God for the purpose of delivering His messages, filling His commands, and worshiping Him. Their purpose is also to protect the believers. The believers today are in the middle of a spiritual war that requires the skill and power of unknown numbers of angels.

God also communicates with Christian through dreams.

Joel 2:28 reads, "And it shall come to pass afterward, that I will pour out my spirit upon all flesh; and your sons and your daughters shall prophesy, your old men shall dream dreams, your young men shall see visions."

God will create dreams and visions for men that are for His purpose and kingdom. These dreams are supported by His word and the Holy Bible. Dreams from God may redirect or refocus a believer in many different ways. Today, living in a fast paced world with many demands and distractions, requires a Christian to stop and take the time to document God's messages and give thanks. It is always important before taking any action to ensure that this action is based on sound biblical teaching.

God uses nature as a messenger for His love for us.

God has created all that is seen and unseen. He created the entire universe and all that it contains. He created a rare and very beautiful planet called earth. And, on this incredibility beautiful planet earth He created man and woman in His own image. He blessed man and woman and allowed them to multiply.

God's message of love, grace, and mercy is displayed each day in His creation of nature. We see God's beauty in the skies, in the snow that blows in the mountains tops, in the fields of flowers that dance in the wind, and in the sunrise that reflects on the oceans and lakes in a rainbow of colors each day. God is faithful.

God's messengers are with the Christian each and every day. They relay God's blessings of peace, comfort, and remind all Christians that they are not alone. God's love approaches all men with the free gift of salvation.

Bibliography

Buswell, James Oliver, Jr. *Problems in the Prayer Life: From a Pastor's Question Box.* Chicago: The Bible Institute, 1928.
Brenton, Lancelot C. *The Septuagint with Apocrypha: Greek and English.* Hendrickson, 1986.
Bruce, Alexander Balmain. *Training of the Twelve.* Keats, 1979.
Bruner, Frederick Dale. *Matthew: A Commentary.* Cambridge: Eerdmans, 2004.
Edersheim, Rev. D. *Sketches of Jewish Social Life in the Day of Christ.* Hodder & Stoughton, 1989.
Geikie, Cunningham. *The Life and Words of Christ.* New York: Appleton, 1879.
Lewis, C. S. *Miracles.* San Francisco: Harper One, 2000.
Ryle, J. C. *Holiness.* Renaissance Classics, 2012.
Spurgeon, Charles H. *Spurgeon's Sermon Notes: Over 250 Sermons including Notes, Commentary and Illustrations.* David Otis Fuller, ed. Grand Rapids: Mt Kregel, 1990.
Webster, Douglas D. *Finding Spiritual Direction.* InterVarsity Press, 1991.

www.ingramcontent.com/pod-product-compliance
Lightning Source LLC
Chambersburg PA
CBHW072137160426
43197CB00012B/2140